D1799480

A TIME TO LEAVE
THE PLOUGHSHARES

A Time to Leave the Ploughshares

A Gunner Remembers 1917–18

by

WILLIAM CARR

ROBERT HALE · LONDON

Copyright © Elizabeth Marshall 1985
First published in Great Britain 1985

ISBN 0 7090 2317 0

Robert Hale Limited
Clerkenwell House
Clerkenwell Green
London EC1R 0HT

All rights reserved. No part of this publication may be
reproduced, stored in a retrieval system or transmitted in any
form or by any means, electronic, mechanical, photocopying,
recording or otherwise, without the prior permission of the
copyright holder.

Photoset in North Wales by
Derek Doyle & Associates, Mold, Clwyd.
Printed in Great Britain by
St Edmundsbury Press, Bury St Edmunds, Suffolk.
Bound by Woolnough Bookbinding Limited.

Contents

List of Illustrations

PICTURE CREDITS

Courtesy of the Sutherland family, 2; the Imperial War Museum, 4-13; all other pictures are the author's. Gardner's sketches were photographed by Clark of Laurencekirk.

MAPS

Editor's Preface

"Have you forgotten yet?...
Look down, and swear by the slain of the War that you'll never forget."
                                                        Siegfried Sassoon
                                                        Aftermath
                                                        March 1919

Seventy years ago thousands of ordinary men were pouring into France to fight, unaware of the terrible ordeal ahead. Soon they would be facing the most appalling holocaust of death and destruction. Those who survived could never forget – the horrifying experience was seared into their memory.

I had always known that my father, William Carr, had many recollections of the First World War but it was not until after he was widowed when I took him, aged ninety-two, to France to revisit the battlefields that I realized how extensive those memories were. He located gun sites occupied by his battery and described in minute detail what had happened there so long ago. Feeling strongly that such vivid accounts should be preserved I persuaded him to record a series of tapes and later to write about the actions in which he fought.

He had not kept diaries and none of his letters home have survived. Yet the more I asked him to fill in the details, the more he was forthcoming. Indeed there was almost enough for two books. To edit the material I had to select and then arrange it in chronological order and verify its accuracy; always of course in close consultation with the author. An initial search in the Public Record Office for the war diaries of the author's brigade was not successful. However, a wider study embracing general and regimental histories (some of which I have appended as a bibliography) progressively confirmed the tale to

9

a remarkable degree. Much later, after the script had been completed, I finally found copies of some of the relevant brigade diaries in the library of the Royal Artillery Institution, where Brigadier R.J. Lewendon also drew my attention to the papers of General Uniacke. These papers contain an account of an action of the author's battery on the 30 November 1917 at Cambrai during which they prevented a German advance on a vital route. It was interesting to note that the author's version in this book of the part he played in that action is the modest one.

Although the book did not set out to be a military history it does contain much first-hand information of interest to the historian. Foremost it is the personal narrative of one man who survived the First World War; one of the dwindling band of veterans for whom Siegfried Sassoon's plea was needless: "Swear by the slain of the War that you'll never forget" – they found it impossible to forget.

We should like to record our gratitude to the many people who have helped during the writing of this book. In particular, we should like to thank John Ellis for his encouragement, and for kindly agreeing to write a Foreword. For permission to reproduce extracts from *The Grey Wave*, by Arthur Hamilton Gibbs, we are grateful to Hutchinson Ltd. We would like to thank the Sutherland family for the photograph of 'The Major', and the Imperial War Museum for several of the other photographs. For their willing co-operation we are much indebted to the staffs of the Imperial War Museum, the library of the Royal Artillery Institution and the Public Record Office, and many other public libraries, especially Northwich Library, Cheshire. We must also thank the several willing helpers who have patiently typed and retyped successive drafts. Finally, I personally would like to thank my own family for their support and encouragement, especially those who read, checked and by suggestion improved the manuscript.

Elizabeth Marshall, 1985

Foreword

by John Ellis

The appearance of this splendid memoir represents a particularly happy outcome for me in that I was some years ago asked to give my opinion on an earlier draft and say whether I felt it merited publication. One has only to glance at this book to appreciate why my answer was swift and unequivocal. The enthusiasm of one military historian does not, however, cut much ice and it must be made clear that the book's actual publication owes much to a literary agent, John Parker, and to Robert Hale themselves, and most of all to William Carr's daughter, Elizabeth Marshall, whose editorial skills and tireless search for historical truth were deft secateurs to the flowerings of her father's astounding memory.

But the story is William Carr's alone. Here in terse, unvarnished terms is the reality of the Western Front. Here, recorded in remarkable detail is the day to day life of a field artillery unit in the First World War, allowing the reader to share fully in the exertions of a strenuous night march, a prolonged barrage, the digging of trenches and gun positions, as well as to gain a very clear understanding of the more technical aspects of a gunner's job. And here too is convincing proof that artillery men were front-line soldiers. William Carr did not join 169 Brigade RFA until June 1917 yet several times he was subjected to savage counter-barrage, once was strafed from the air, once had to break through virtual encirclement to

11

rejoin his own unit, and twice was obliged to fire over open sites at an enemy only a few yards distant.

With recourse neither to excessive sentimentality nor to an obsessive emphasis upon the 'horrors of war', the author calmly yet remorselessly brings us face to face with the extremes of fatigue, hunger, fear, blood-lust, grief and compassion that were the stock spectrum of sensation and emotion in Flander's fields. Others have told us of these outer limits of the human experience but few other than William Carr have so convincingly shown how they were simply the reactions of ordinary, reasonable, peace-loving men suddenly pitched into a world whose only rationale was an utterly brutal material monomania and where the only freedom was to kill or be killed. All who read this book will be deeply thankful that William Carr was spared to return to the ploughshares he so loved and to now remind us, with the wise compassion of experience, of the abyss before which mankind still teeters.

John Ellis, Manchester, 1985

Introduction

I suppose for me the story starts in January 1916 – the scene, Lincoln's Inn. I stood before three Army officers seated behind a table:

"What games did you play at school?"

"We didn't play games, Sir."

"You didn't play games?"

The officers stared at me in disbelief.

In no time at all I was outside the door passing the queue of men waiting to be interviewed for commissions.

I felt then that I had little chance of being accepted. The brass hats had asked me a lot of questions and given me a fair enough hearing, but it was obvious that they considered my lack of games experience a serious handicap. Naturally, I was disappointed at the way the interview had gone but wasn't unduly upset.

As I left the peaceful gardens of the Inns of Court my thoughts dwelt on the war and the whole question of joining up. I had no great pretence of patriotism and having recently graduated from Aberdeen University at the mature age of thirty, regarded the war as an obstacle in the path of my hard-earned career. However, during 1915 one after another of my friends had been killed in France and it was the death of my student friend Knochandu from the place of that name on Speyside which finally brought me to a decision. I joined up not so much to fight for King and Country but in the belief that if sufficient numbers enlisted, the war would be won and the terrible losses stopped. For this reason I'd felt that it was my duty to go, and I still felt the same way, despite the disdain of the brass hats.

For me, enlisting had been more difficult because in order to pass the fitness tests I'd had to undergo an operation for varicocele. In the first place I'd had to find the money to pay for the operation and then it had proved quite difficult to find a surgeon, as all medical services were overloaded by war wounded. My father had helped with the finance and eventually our family doctor had found a surgeon who was prepared to travel the twenty miles from Aberdeen to my home south of Stonehaven, a farm called Barras. The operation was performed satisfactorily on the scrubbed kitchen table, brought into the drawing room, cleared of its furnishings for the event.

After six months' convalescence I had been recommended for a commission and this had resulted in the interview from which I was now returning, troubled mainly by the thought that an unsuccessful outcome would let down my kindly sponsor.

Not in any way regarding myself as a fighting man I was in no hurry to go out to France and as I walked through the streets of London awaiting the departure of the night express to Scotland I made a decision I was later to regret. If my application for a commission was rejected I would wait to be called up, the Derby scheme being about to make compulsory the call-up of all fit men of military age. A few extra weeks on the farm, I reasoned, could be spent giving much needed help to finish the ploughing. I didn't appreciate then how much I would come to resent the slur of being called a Derby boy.

I don't remember catching the train nor the journey to Stonehaven but I was met by my brother John with his newly acquired second-hand motor car, which was, I believe, a Vauxhall Prince Henry. He'd bought it in Aberdeen and had driven straight back to Barras, although he'd never driven a car before in his life. Now he took me back by the coast road, up the Bervie Brae and past the Black Hill, with its rounded summit where in the fullness of time the silhouette of a sombre

14

arched monument would rivet the eye, a stark memorial to the war dead.

As we sped southwards past the craggy fortress of Dunnottar, I wondered what my parents would say. They would feel my departure for the war very deeply. My youngest brother, Henry had been the first to go. Comparatively lucky, he'd been wounded and discharged. They could not expect to be so fortunate a second time. Looking out across the North Sea, I remembered how, as a boy, I had been scolded for climbing down the steep cliffs to fish from dangerous rocks. My mother would be especially anxious. At Mill of Uras we turned inland over Gregory's Brae, then on up the last mile to Barras.

It was a week or more before I received the formal rejection of my application for a commission. Then a few days later another letter arrived and this one I had not anticipated. The handwriting was unfamiliar. As I opened the envelope out fluttered a white feather, the symbol of cowardice. During the First World War white feathers were sent to men who had failed to enlist by well-meaning but misguided ladies who felt they were doing their bit for King and Country by rounding up the cowards. As well as anonymously sending the feathers by post, the ladies would stand in the city streets handing them out to men who were not in uniform. It was a cruel practice as a feather was often received by a man who had been wounded and was now in civies or had some other good reason for not being in uniform. I had no idea who sent the white feather. It must have been some slight lady acquaintance and the incident shouldn't really have bothered me but it did; I felt very hurt indeed.

However, a few days later a much more significant event occurred at Barras. This was the arrival of a Mogul tractor imported by the American International Harvester Company. No other farm in the district had a tractor; indeed, there were very few anywhere in Britain. It was typical of my brothers to try one. Then there were no special tractor ploughs so using a chain we fixed an ordinary horse plough behind the tractor.

During eleven years as a farm worker I had won many prizes for ploughing so I was given the task of holding the plough. I soon found that a tractor could not be controlled like my old horses, Prince and Rose, and the furrows I made were somewhat erratic. However, we were convinced that ploughing and harrowing could be done more speedily than with horses and decided to persevere with the tractor.

But soon it was time to leave the ploughshares. The postie delivered my call-up papers with an instruction to report to Castlehill Barracks, Aberdeen, in a fortnight's time.

The evening before my departure my beloved Daisy cycled over to Barras as soon as she had finished her day's work at school. We had been engaged for nearly five years and it had been for her that I had left Barras to enrol at university as we had felt that the farm was not sufficiently prosperous to support us all. Later that night we cycled back together down the Smithy Road. We had a short walk on Kinneff Hill where we had done our courting, we didn't know what to say. I took her to her digs and kissed her goodbye at the door.

There was little fuss about my departure; another man off to the war – it was all too common an occurrence. At Barras there was much leg pulling, advice about wearing the kilt and other jokes – a brave attempt to hide the anxiety they all felt. Like me they assumed I would be put into the Gordons, an infantry regiment – passport to the trenches and death.

John took me to Aberdeen in the Vauxhall. I do not recall the journey but I imagine I was not different from other men leaving home to go to war, gazing hard at the familiar places to keep them fresh in mind – the whin bushes where I'd hunted with my shot-gun; the Swiney burn where I'd guddled trout; a last look at Barras from Gregory's Brae; the Mill of Uras dam where I'd caught my first trout on a fly, and on the main road, the smithy where I'd taken my ploughshares be sharpened.

I cannot tell you what my thoughts were as we sped along the coast road, then round the sharp corner by the Black Hill, with Stonehaven bay spread out below us; or what my feelings were as we went down the Bervie Brae through the town and up the Cowie Brae. All I know is that someone up there must have been watching over me as I left these familiar places. For looking back, what strikes me now as I recall my time in the Army, is my extraordinary luck. Time and again sheer chance deemed that I would survive to tell the tale.

John put me down near the barracks. I was directed to a hall where several young lads stood in an anxious group making subdued conversation. In due course a sergeant appeared. I cannot remember what he said but the gist of it was that all recruits who reported that day were to be posted to the Royal Field Artillery. My good luck had begun.

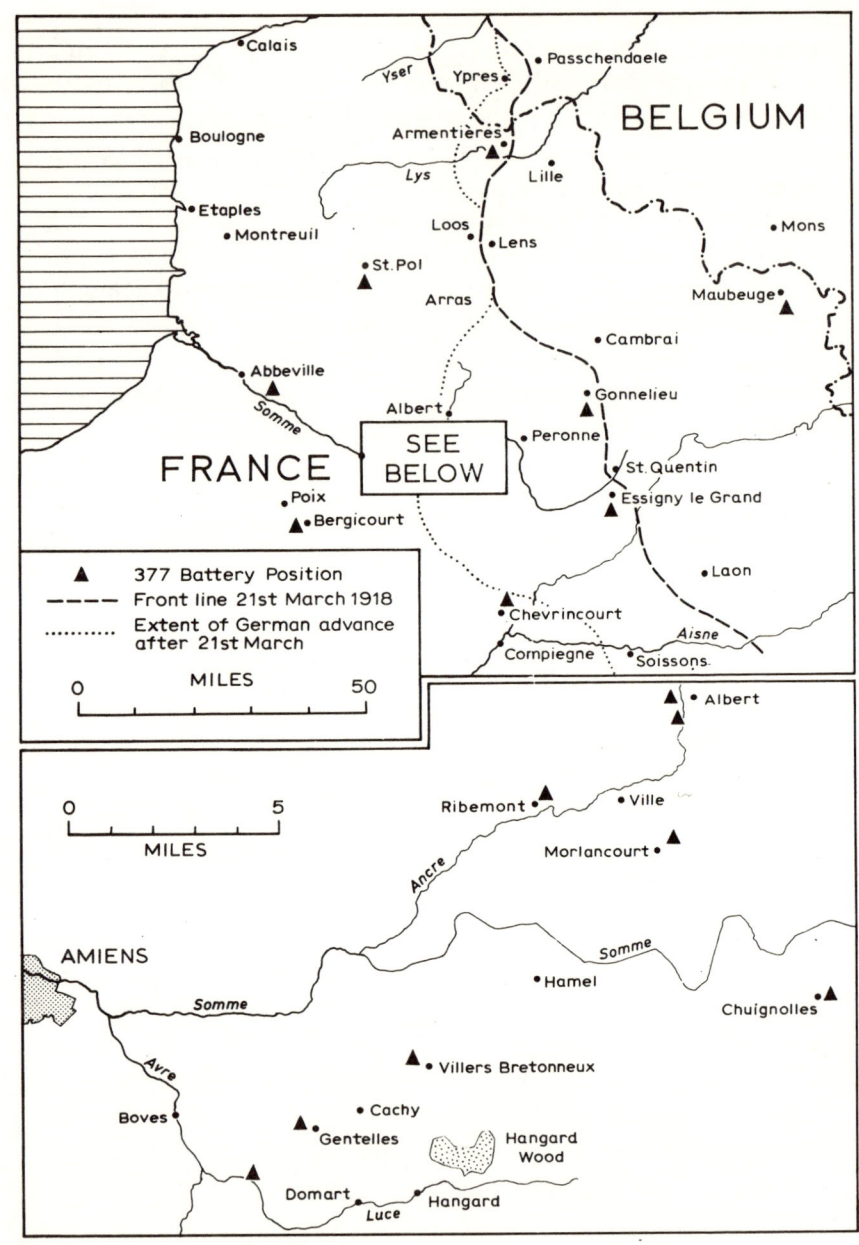

377 Battery Positions in France, 1917 and 1918

18

1

Gun Line

It was in fact a year before I reached the gun line. After completing a period of training at Bicton Camp, Luton, we had arrived at the station en route for France when at the last minute an adjutant appeared and announced that a number of men were to fall out and return to camp to form a headquarter's staff. The first name on the list was Gunner Carr. I was bitterly disappointed but I should have got down on my knees and thanked the Almighty for I missed the Somme.

We were at Luton for weeks but the headquarter's staff never materialized, so that all of us who had returned feared that we might be trapped there for the duration. Then one of us was recommended for a commission and persuaded all the rest to apply. The upshot was that five of us were accepted to train for commissions. Expecting an immediate posting we were increasingly frustrated as still nothing happened. In fact it was six months later in February 1917, when our orders came through to report to the officer training camp at Topsham Barracks, Exeter. By the end of May we had completed our training and I was commissioned Second Lieutenant in the 3/3 London Brigade Royal Field Artillery. There was then a week's embarkation leave which I spent at Barras with my wife Daisy whom I had married just before I was due to leave for France the first time. On returning from Scotland I received my posting to 169 Army Brigade RFA which had recently taken over part of the line south of Armentières. My friends Faircloth and Carter received the same posting.

We crossed the Channel from Folkestone to Boulogne on 6 June 1917 and travelled by train to Bailleul where we checked into an hotel for the night.

What a date to arrive! Bailleul is a few miles south-west of Messines where the Germans were established on a low ridge from which they could observe all British movement to the rear of Ypres. Before launching a new offensive on the Ypres front it was necessary for the British to capture this position and by 6 June preparations were complete. During the last ten days the Artillery in close cooperation with the Royal Flying Corps had carried out a preliminary bombardment and, unknown to the Germans, sappers had for weeks been tunnelling deeply under the ridge to place mines containing many tons of explosives.

All this was quite unknown to us as we went to bed in our hotel, very excited about being in France at last, and wondering what the next day would bring. We hadn't long to wait. Just after 3 a.m. the mines were exploded and, under cover of a creeping barrage, infantry together with a number of tanks, stormed the position. When I tell you that the explosions were heard in London and that never before had such a mass of artillery been concentrated on so narrow a section, you can imagine we had something of a shock awakening. No wonder the hotel was shaken to its foundations and the maids screamed, "Sales Boches". We certainly thought we'd be in action all too soon and for the first time I was worried about what might happen.

We waited in the hotel until afternoon when a wagon arrived from 169 Brigade to take us and our kit to Brigade Headquarters, at Fleurbaix, near Armentières. It was only a short journey but it took a long time with many hold-ups to allow the passage of both horse drawn and motorized vehicles moving to the front. All the time we could hear the vicious strafe on the ridge. The whole area seemed to be lit up with constant gun flashes and there was no mistaking the noise of the guns. I felt frightened – very frightened indeed. In fact it was the only time I felt frightened in this way during the war. In those days there were few films, no television and no radio. I had only a picture-book idea of what war was like. Now here it was – the real thing.

We cheered up a little when we reached Headquarters where we were met by the Colonel, a pleasant, rather oldish man. I think he had been a regular soldier, retired before the war but recalled for active service. He welcomed us, introduced us to the Headquarters' staff and we had a meal together in the mess.

After dinner Faircloth was sent to join 379 Battery and Carter went to 376. I was rather worried about being left behind but as I watched the gun flashes and listened to the din, at the same time I was quite relieved not to be thrown into action straightaway.

In fact what I was witnessing in the distance was the end of the first day of an operation which had been organised by Major-General Sir Herbert Plumer and his staff. This was a real British success story. When I say British I must make it quite clear that British in those days was taken to include Australians, Canadians, New Zealanders, South Africans – everyone from the Empire. Here it had been an Australian division under Monash and a New Zealand division which had played the major role.

Quite early in the morning these divisions had taken their objectives and then, later in the day, made further gains. This was in fact the brilliant prelude to the Third Battle of Ypres. Once again I must emphasize that all I knew was that there was a battle going on and it wasn't far away. I can't remember where I slept at HQ, only that wherever it was, I felt very much alone.

Next day the Colonel told me to report to 377 Battery. He informed me that its commanding officer was a Major Neil Sutherland who, when he'd joined up, had been a Minister of the Scottish Kirk in Edinburgh. Then he added that as 377 was known as the Scots Battery I should feel quite at home there.

My kit was bundled into a mess cart and we drove more than a mile to Rue Flourie farm, near Bois Grenier, where 377 Battery was established a mile behind the front line. The countryside was flat, broken only by lines of Lombardy poplars. Rue Flourie appeared, a single storeyed brick farmhouse with a range of out-buildings. There were sheets of corrugated iron patching the roof and there were broken panes in the windows but on the whole it didn't seem too badly knocked about.

Major Sutherland met me at the door and welcomed me to 377 Battery. Inside I met Smith and Martin, two of the subalterns. Tumblers appeared and Martin pulled a bottle of Scotch out of a case on the floor. They drank my health and wished me luck with the Battery and during the ensuing conversation I learned that Smith and Martin also came from Edinburgh and that Smith had recently graduated at the university.

For the rest of the morning the Major spent his time putting me in the picture. He told me that as 169 was an Army Field Artillery Brigade it didn't belong to any division, which meant that it could be moved from one front to another as required. We were on the "Leys" front, the river Leys being two miles behind the position of the battery. Our wagon lines were established on the river bank, side by side with those of 379 Battery – a battery with which we would be closely associated in the future.

I was shown the battery map, marked off in 1,000-yard squares with 100-yard marks round the sides. The position of 377 was shown with a line drawn to connect it with a wrecked house on the other side of the intricate network of trenches because our aiming posts were registered on this building, with the sights at O. The Major set a protractor on this line and with a gut string showed how easy it was to give a switch to right or left of the target. Then I was shown the battery box, a small black tin chest which contained secret orders and code words, and I was introduced to some of the paperwork, in particular the reports which I would have to submit when on Observation Post (OP) duty.

The Major summoned a man from the kitchen and told him he was to be my batman. The man was slight of build and seemed shy and retiring, obviously he regarded the job of batman with no great enthusiasm and looking back I can appreciate that it must have been very disappointing for a man to set out to fight for King and Country and find himself relegated to the role of servant. Particularly hard to be servant to an ordinary, rather elderly fellow as I must have appeared to him. The man, remembered by me as Duncan, became a valued friend and assistant.

The Major showed me the bedroom I would share with him, telling me the only other was occupied by Smith and Martin. We had a concoction of stewed bully beef and potatoes for lunch after which Smith took me to see the guns of the right section and centre section which were in the remains of a stable and looseboxes. The original roof had disappeared but iron rails on top were covered with a thick layer of concrete and the walls were reinforced. The guns sat between partitions, their muzzles projecting through the holes towards the orchard. I noticed the aiming posts set in the ground ahead of each gun. Shells were stacked by the guns. At the near end, Martin, the officer on duty, sat at a table with a battery map and telephone. He was accompanied by NCOs and gunners. Smith introduced me to the NCOs but I had difficulty in getting them to talk – obviously I was being given the "once over".

The Major himself showed me the OP which was in a large barn at one end of which there was a twelve-foot iron ladder to a steel box, big enough to hold two men. From it we could see over our trenches though not into them. There was a mass of barbed wire in front and in places we could see the enemy line. There was a clear view of the slope of the Aubers Ridge and there were a number of ruined farms and cottages. The Major pointed out the ruin on which our guns were registered which earlier he had shown me on the battery map. When I studied it through my field glasses it looked quite near. It was interesting to see how the black wooden cruck frame remained standing while the rest of the building was little more than a heap of rubble.

Two signallers had followed us into the building and taken up positions at the bottom of the ladder. The Major ordered: "Centre section prepare for action."

Within minutes the reply came back from the guns.

"Ready Sir."

The Major ordered zero (on aiming posts) fire one round of HE (high explosive) at range of 3020. The blast from the guns shook the OP and we watched one shell land just over the wrecked building and the other a few yards to the left of it.

"Now you have a go," said the Major.

He pointed out another ruin to the left and further away. I set my protractor on the map which was in front of us and ordered 2 degrees 50 minutes left, range 4050, one round HE, fire when ready. The shells landed to the right and beyond the ruin. I made my correction ordering 30 minutes left and drop 100. This time the shells landed quite near the target.

The Major emphasized that the main task of the officer on OP duty was to look out for SOS rockets. These were distress flares sent up by our infantry when they were being attacked and wished us to fire on the oncoming enemy and his front line trenches. The rockets, always of a distinguishing colour, were red while we were at Armentières. When an "SOS" signal was seen the Observation Officer had to shout "SOS" to the signallers who would transmit this to the officer at the guns. There was no need to align the guns as they were normally left on SOS lines, that is trained on a fifty-yard stretch of enemy front line trenches or on the wire just in front of them. The Major warned that we might come under fire, and if the line to the Battery was cut then the officer on OP duty was responsible for maintaining communications.

The Major next advised me to visit the left section commanded by Crombie, the senior subaltern, whose guns were hidden in the corner of a small field about four hundred yards behind Rue Flourie. Despite his name Crombie was the only English officer in the Battery. He was about twenty-seven, very friendly, but rather a serious fellow who lived alone in a rickety old gipsy caravan by his guns. Rather bad luck being all by himself I thought but, as I discovered later, this arrangement suited him very well. He was a teetotaller and as we Scots enjoyed a dram he was rather the odd man out.

I had a good look round and noted the deep ditches which divided the fields before returning to the mess where we were joined by the second-in-command, Captain Gardner. In civilian life he'd been an artist and I learned that he had designed the interior decorations of the crack Cunard liners *Mauretania* and *Lusitania*. Gardner was in charge of the wagon line where all supplies and services were kept and also our horses and mules which were tethered in the open. The wagon line was two miles back, out of range of the enemy's field artillery, though not of his long-range guns.

Next day I was taken down to Battalion HQ in the trenches and was introduced to the Colonel and his officers. After a drink in their mess, one of the officers took me along the trenches which had names like Snipers' Alley, Salop Avenue, Paradise Alley and Wine Avenue.

From the HQ mess he led me along a communication trench to the front line proper. The trenches proceeded in a zig-zag fashion to give protection from enfilade fire during enemy raids. These were only two or three feet in the ground, with wooden duck boards laid at the bottom. Walls back and front were built up with sandbags making a parapet seven or more feet high. In the front line trench there were a series of bays with fire steps at regular intervals. At one place my guide took me to a periscope. I could see a mass of rusty barbed wire and the enemy parapet beyond but I couldn't detect any sign of life. It was a fearful place and I felt very lucky that my duty lay nearly a mile away at the gun line.

After a few days I was completely at home in 377 Battery

and soon Barras, and the life I'd left behind, seemed years away. I doubt if I realized at the time how lucky I was to be sent to 377 not only because it was the Scots Battery but because at least two of the subalterns were older than those of most other batteries where anyone over twenty-five was commonly regarded by the confident young subalterns as a liability, someone who 'had to be carried'. At thirty-three my arrival in their midst would have been regarded as a disaster. As it was, I couldn't have chosen a happier battery or friendlier fellow officers. I even acquired a nick name. The Major christened me 'Carlos' and my real name was never used.

The Major was an exceptional commanding officer, full of energy and enthusiasm, able to get the maximum amount of respect and cooperation from subalterns and men with the minimum amount of formality. He had a delightful sense of humour as you will learn from my story. He implied that he was about my age but I know now that he was a few years younger.

I became well acquainted with all the NCOs and gunners but I remember few names, probably because we always called them "Sergeant" or "Bombardier" or "Gunner". I particularly remember the sergeants of Crombie's section, the one which was later to be mine. I often walked over the fields to stretch my legs after a night on OP duty and, when I reached the guns of the left section, I had a chat with Sergeant Gray and another sergeant whose name I remember as Watson. Sergeant Gray was an athletic down to earth Glaswegian, enterprising and quick witted. I don't remember his civilian job but he was a keen amateur footballer, playing for Queen's Park, then one of the top Scottish teams, its home ground being Hampden Park. Sergeant Watson, in contrast, was the intellectual artistic type. A delightful charming man, he'd been a music master at a Glasgow school.

Of the servants in the mess, apart from Duncan, the one I particularly recall was the Major's batman, a tough lively little Scot from the Fife coalfields. He'd won prizes for hewing more coal on a shift than anyone else in the mine. He was a character of outsize proportions with a delightful sense of humour like his Major. He was always respectful but I don't believe he was ever subservient or overawed whoever visited the mess.

I remember also Whittaker, one of our signallers, who had been a seaman and had exceptionally good eyesight. At considerable distance he could detect the slightest movement or change of form. Often when on OP duty I got him to confirm what I thought I'd seen beyond the enemy trenches.

At Rue Flourie we were in the enviable position of being on what was known as a "quiet front". Whenever possible the enemy in the trenches opposite was content to lie low providing we did the same. It was a case of live and let live. But sometimes higher command decreed otherwise. The enemy would bring up big guns on the railway just south of Lille and have a go at us while we in our turn fired to support our infantry when they were ordered to raid enemy trenches with the object of gaining information on troop deployment. On these occasions it was customary for an officer of the supporting artillery to go over the top with the infantry; the task never fell to me but I recall a very shaken Smith shocking us with his account of this experience.

We soon learnt to distinguish between the various German shells. There were the big 5.9s which took a steep curve in flight giving an unmistakable noisy approach which gave ample time to take cover. The 4.2s were similar but because they were smaller we could not hear them so easily. Lastly there were the HVs (high velocity shells) known as pip squeaks which were fired from a smaller version of our own field-gun and sped towards us following a much lower trajectory giving little or no warning. The shells which pounded Rue Flourie were of three types: HE (high explosive) which burst when they touched the ground; shrapnel, which the gunners set with fuses to burst in the air in order to hit a human target with bullet or flying pieces of metal; and shells filled with the dreaded mustard gas which lingered long after they had hit our position.

27

There were periods which were comparatively trouble free and not being in charge of a section I had a certain amount of spare time which I used to make myself thoroughly familiar with every aspect of gunnery. Using a map and compass I'd register imaginary targets, take "back bearings" on the aiming post in front of a gun and carry out other procedures which later I would use in the heat of battle. Frequently I had practice shoots. I cannot over emphasize how valuable the opportunity to acquire this expertise was to prove in the months ahead.

My five months at Rue Flourie remain clearly in mind. I remember the moment when for the first time in France I stood behind guns counting down to zero. I remember countless incidents when German shells hit our position and I remember how my own personal luck continued when I came under machine-gun fire for the first time, and again one day when about to go up in a balloon on observation duty I was recalled at the last minute only to see later the balloon shot down in flames. I remember also the lighter side, particularly Gardner's birthday party, when, after a celebratory dinner in our mess the Major sent to the wagon line for his white charger which he then rode up and down the lane scattering a platoon of infantry men and then scattering them again as laughingly they reformed and how to the great delight of our gunners who were watching at a discreet distance one of the infantrymen yelled:

"Look out here comes the bugger again!"

Compared with what happened later, this summer of 1917 was quite tolerable though danger always threatened and we were lucky to escape casualties, but as we listened to the continual noise of gunfire from Ypres where a deadly struggle had raged since Messines we began to feel, 'it won't happen to us'.

In the farmhouse officers and men lived under cover or in the buildings. We were as comfortable as possible, pinning photographs on the wall, supplementing our rations by buying food and wine in Armentières. In the evening we wound up

Smith's gramophone playing over and over again our favourite record "Caprice Venois". I don't remember any other musical instruments but the men sang; often coming from their quarters we heard their own versions of the popular songs of the day. Not surprisingly since Gardner's birthday party one of the most popular had been "The Galloping Major".

In September 1917 our quiet life came to an end as the Hun attacked Armentières. Thousands of gas shells, incendiaries and HEs almost reduced the town to rubble. Those citizens who escaped death fled. Many shells fell near our position and often we were forced to wear gas masks but still we escaped injury.

Each night during the Hun's attack on Armentières there was intense activity behind the enemy lines as he brought up ammunition and supplies. Our main task was to harass all roads leading to the front. It was an interesting game trying to outwit the Hun who'd been typically unimaginative in his attacks on us, pounding the same spot with meticulous regularity. Studying the map we'd move from target to target, varying our timing and paying attention to cross roads further back as well as those near the front. I couldn't help sympathizing with Jerry drivers who were in charge of wagons and horses and was glad that our roles were not reversed. We kept up this harassment for about twenty days until the front became quiet again.

With Armentières in ruins our diet became less varied so it was understandable that when one of our horses fell in a shell hole, broke a leg, and had to be shot, Sergeant Gray bled the animal and within a day or two had all the men enjoying tasty steaks. Alas, unlike the Second World War, to eat horsemeat was against Army regulations and when the Major heard what had happened he had no alternative but to order that the remainder be destroyed. It was the only upset I can remember in the usual amicable relationship between the Major and the gunners.

However soon after this incident, the Major went into

Armentières to reconnoitre a possible new position for the Battery. When he returned he sent for me. "Carlos," he said, "You and I will do a raid tonight." He paused long enough for me to have visions of blacking my face and going over the top through the wire. Then he went on. "I've found some bee hives in a garden. Arrange for two signallers to come with us, we'll go to collect the honey. Be ready to start at ten p.m."

That night when it was dark we made a two-mile trek cross country to the garden, keeping a low profile to avoid military police for there were heavy penalties for looting. As we cut into the bee hives we were stung from head to foot. After much cursing and swearing we managed to fill two dixies with honeycombs, enough to give officers and men a treat. We returned without incident.

Next morning the Major told me to take a jar of honey to the Colonel at HQ and describe the raid on a regulation report. I duly wrote this out giving the map square of the target. I reported that we found the enemy buzzing with activity, present in enormous numbers and that we inflicted heavy casualties. The Colonel laughed when he read it and asked for more details. He was delighted to have the honey. But if we had been caught by the military police it would have been very different.

Our time at Rue Flourie was coming to an end. Soon there would be no time for frivolities. It was a very wet autumn and we were sorry for the infantry in front when their trenches filled with water. Sometime in October our friends were replaced by a Portuguese division and it was rumoured that 169 Brigade was to go north to Ypres. We had heard of the conditions there, the appalling mud, lack of cover and ceaseless rain of gas shells.

It was early November. As we waited fearing the worst what we didn't know was that the Third Battle of Ypres which had begun so hopefully with Messines was already coming to an end with the most terrible engagement of the First World War –

pack up and be ready by dark next evening – our destination was top secret. We were to travel south.

2

Night Journey

Just before the order came through that we were to be ready to move within twenty-four hours, we learned that Crombie was to be promoted to Captain and sent to another brigade, and I was to take his place in charge of the left section. I felt that it was quite enough to cope with the responsibility of commanding a section without the complications of a move. I'd never been with a brigade on the road before. In fact, I'd never even visited the wagon line where our horses and mules were kept in the open. Now we had to be mobile in a matter of hours. I was very worried.

Each battery of a brigade was more or less self-sufficient and therefore everywhere it went it took along not only guns and ammunition but also a great deal of paraphernalia; our section carried its share. As well as the eighteen-pounders, we had a Lewis gun and a few rifles, supposedly to use for defence should we be overrun. There was equipment for the maintenance of guns and transport, and for the care of horses. Then there was the signallers' equipment such as lines, lamps and flags. Other items I recall were picks, shovels, axes, ropes, horse rugs and canvas for bivouac shelters. There was a separate wagon for cooking stoves and utensils. I do remember that very little food was taken, for us or the horses, and that I was surprised that there was no issue of iron rations. There were also our personal belongings, and as the Brigade had been at Rue Flourie for five months we had accumulated far more than the regulation kit.

Finally, we had to find a place for the camouflage nets which had been issued at the last minute. We didn't know where to put them but they ended up on the gun limbers – the correct place as it turned out.

Thank goodness only minor things went wrong with the left section's preparations. The smooth operation was due mainly to the hard work of Sergeant Watson and Sergeant Gray who had moved with the Brigade from its formation in Ireland to England and from England to France and knew exactly what to do. They worked like Trojans themselves and, with good humour and tact, got everybody moving at the double.

We had to be ready for inspection by the Major two hours before we were due to join the rest of the Brigade. To my great relief we made it. No fault was found except for a personal matter which took me rather by surprise. The Major who had always dealt with me quite informally now suddenly shouted at me as if we were on the barrack square.

"Why aren't you wearing the shoulder strap of your Sam Browne?"

I looked at him in amazement. We had never bothered to wear our shoulder straps at Rue Flourie and I'd forgotten all about it.

Having accumulated quite a few extras at Rue Flourie we were short of transport. Just before we left, the Colonel – and I think the Major had a hand in it – decided that we should bring along the gipsy caravan which I had inherited from the teetotal Crombie. With a nice touch of irony, they decided that each battery would contribute a case of whisky and that it would serve as a temporary brigade mess to receive visiting senior officers. I was to bring the caravan along behind the left section.

I didn't think the damned thing would stand the journey. It was picturesque – but very old and rickety and looked as if it hadn't been moved for years. I would have liked to remove the wheels and soak them in a pond for a day or two to make the felloes fit more tightly, but there wasn't time for that. We loaded the whisky, and a pair of horses pulled off with the ancient vehicle creaking and groaning behind.

By nightfall the Brigade had assembled. It was an impressive spectacle – all guns, limbers, GS (General Service) wagons, men on horseback and on foot manoeuvring into position in the fading light to make a queue a mile long waiting to move off. The HQ staff led, followed by the four batteries, each in its allotted position. Our 377 Battery brought up the rear. I rode in front of the left section which was last of all, with the rickety caravan right at the back.

I remember the air of excitement and expectancy with an undercurrent of anxiety and foreboding. The subalterns knew we were travelling south – the safer direction, or so we thought. We knew we were to be on the move during the next four or five nights and we knew we were to sleep by day in billets to be found in villages and farm buildings, but it had been emphasized that the utmost secrecy was to be maintained. We did not know where we were going or what our next assignment was to be.

I was glad that we were travelling by night and that our journey was being concealed from the Germans. I couldn't help remembering, when the boot was on the other foot, how we had plastered the roads as they brought up their supplies during their attack on Armentières. I offered up a thankful prayer that I wasn't a driver, not because I disliked looking after horses, but because I now realized how vulnerable the drivers would be if we were under fire when on the move. Each driver rode on the left horse of a pair and was expected to stay there whatever happened. There was no possibility of a quick dive into the ditch.

We must have been travelling south from Armentières and keeping more or less parallel to the line passing west of Vimy Ridge which the British had held since April when it had been captured by the Canadians. We could see very little of the countryside in the dark. There were still a few inhabitants in the village we passed through, although many buildings had suffered from shelling. Progress was slow; our estimated speed was two-and-a-half miles per hour, and we rarely covered more than fifteen miles in any one night.

When on the move, the drivers were on horseback with the spare drivers and gunners perched on the GS wagons. A few gunners could ride on ammunition limbers, but no one rode on gun limbers. Most preferred to walk part of the time to relieve the cramp which developed all too soon. There was no attempt to maintain strict discipline. We were so spread out that the men rarely sang. My section alone occupied about 140 yards of the road, quite different from infantry on the march, in which case a whole company covered no more than 125 yards; it was quite easy for them to strike up a song. With us, though, the night air reverberated with the clatter of the iron-shod horses' hooves, the jingle of the harness and the clanking of the wagon wheels.

We had a few organized halts but often small accidents occurred which caused hold-ups in the column. Headquarters organized a billeting party which consisted of an officer and a representative from each battery which went ahead to choose the halting place for our daylight rest. They hadn't much choice and when we arrived it was nearly always a problem to conceal the guns and limbers from enemy planes and disperse ourselves and the horses. More often or not we sheltered in ruined buildings and Duncan would find a corner to put down my valise. Occasionally we all lay beside our horses under the cover of trees with nothing more than a blanket and a groundsheet for protection.

Food was by far our greatest difficulty. There was supposed to be an advance depot from which our QMS (Quarter Master Sergeant) should have been able to collect rations for the men and food for the horses, but on arrival he was invariably told that these supplies had gone astray. There was nothing for it but to turn a blind eye while the men went off to pick up whatever food they could find in the village or beg from the inhabitants still there. They usually fared better than the officers but there wasn't much to be had anyway and all of us, as well as the horses, went hungry.

This was my first experience of shortage of food and it was by no means the last. All we had were a few dry biscuits. We thought that the trouble might be due to being an Army Brigade, not attached to a division. "Nobody's children" – we called ourselves; or maybe the train bringing the food had broken down or been strafed by an enemy plane.

The men complained very little. They were as much concerned about the horses as themselves. All of us tried to make allowances and understand the difficulties. We'd have understood them even better if we'd known what we discovered later on, that we were taking part in one of the most imaginative exercises of the First World War; that on these November nights over 100,000 men and as many horses were on the move. No wonder rations went astray.

I did what I could to see that the men were as comfortable as possible. All had work to do before turning in. Horses went lame or had lost shoes, wagons or limbers needed mechanical attention but worst of all there was the rickety caravan to repair.

As expected the caravan gave trouble. During the first night we were only a mile or two on the way when one of the men reported that it was stranded some distance behind the convoy. I galloped back to find that one of the wheels had collapsed. Returning to my section I took a rope from a GS wagon and went back again to bind up the dislodged felloes to the iron rim, then left the caravan to trail behind.

After each night's journey the caravan needed repairs as the rope with which I'd strapped the felloes to the iron rim was nearly worn through and had to be replaced. This job required a certain amount of skill and practice and there wasn't time to teach anyone else. It was a temporary expedient sometimes carried out on a farm to enable a broken down cart to be wheeled to the smithy for repairs. The men were fascinated, and at first stood round to watch, but soon the novelty wore off and by noon each day I was alone with the decrepit vehicle.

The Colonel heard that we had nearly lost the caravan on the first night. He and the HQ staff were determined that their temporary mess with its precious load should not be left behind. Each night when we were on the move they sent a question down the line.

"Is the caravan all correct?" Gunners and drivers were highly amused for everyone knew what was in the caravan. The question was repeated several times a night. In fact, it became a sort of game to relieve the monotony of the march. We would first hear the question in the distance at the head of the column,

"Is the caravan all correct?"

Translated in places by Scottish voices, "Is the caravan ah richt?"

It got louder and louder as it was repeated down the line finally reaching myself. If all was well I sent the message back, "Yes, the caravan is all correct."

We could hear the reply echoing into the distance, translated again, "Aye, the caravan's ah richt," until it reached the head of the column a mile away. It was a great joke to everyone except me. I could have seen the beastly thing in Timbuctoo.

I well remember the morning we arrived in Arras. Duncan told me he had procured a chicken and that it would be cooked and ready by the time I'd seen to the guns and the horses, "And the caravan," he added.

"Wonderful!"

I was ravenous. I hurried off determined to sort out the problems in record time. All went well until I reached the caravan, then disaster. I found the spokes of one of the wheels were cracked almost beyond repair. It would be very difficult to make it roadworthy. With the thought of the chicken to spur me on, I set to work, but it became more and more obvious that I was fighting a losing battle.

37

After some time the Major appeared; I showed him the spokes.

"Couldn't we possibly load it on a limber?" I pleaded.

"No," he replied. "We haven't got far to go now. Do what you can. If it collapses we'll send back a wagon to collect the contents."

Wearily I carried on. The Major opened the caravan and went inside. Out he came with a bottle of Scotch.

"That'll do man. Off you go and take this with you."

To reach the "mess" I had to walk through a roofless building occupied by one or two of my men. I tried to keep the bottle out of sight but as each resting gunner lifted his head to watch me pass, a broad grin spread over his face.

Now for the chicken! I went into the temporary mess and there was Duncan almost in tears.

"The cook has burned the chicken to a cinder. I can't find a scrap of food anywhere," he wailed.

I was so hungry, absolutely desperate for food. For a moment I was speechless. Then I remembered the whisky.

"Bring me my grog bowl," I said. I opened the bottle and poured myself a very large neat whisky.

Duncan helped me to my valise. I lay down, glanced up at the grey November sky, and straight away fell asleep. Strange to say I felt absolutely OK when Duncan wakened me at 5 p.m.

After leaving Arras we must have turned south-east. There was another night journey, and yet another, but nothing of note happened until we reached our destination before day-break on 16 November.

With hindsight, it is extraordinary to think that neither during the night marches, nor when resting during the daylight, were we aware of the movement of any other unit.

3

The Battle of Cambrai

Prelude

On 16 November we knew we had arrived at our destination but we hadn't the slightest idea where we were and couldn't even make any guesses as all discussion had been banned in the interest of secrecy. There was no sign of the Major who presumably had gone to the new HQ. The wagons and caravan had also departed, leaving us with guns and ammunition.

We couldn't see anything as it wasn't yet light and there was thick mist, but we weren't particularly concerned with our whereabouts. What was far more important was that there was a plentiful supply of food. I was starving and lost no time in tucking into a tin of bully beef and some bread while the cook produced a mug of hot tea. After savouring every morsel all I wanted was a sleep, but first we had to camouflage the guns. The sergeants and I selected a place beside a derelict wall and started to clear away some rubble. Then the Major appeared.

"Carlos," he said. "I've got a job for you. Come over here." We moved out of earshot and he produced a large-scale fighting map which we opened up between us and laid flat on the ground.

"We're here," said the Major, marking our position which was two miles east of Metz en Couture near the Gouzeaucourt-Trescault road.

"I want you to reconnoitre a cross-country route to this position."

He indicated a map square a mile or more away which was east of the Gouzeaucourt-Villers Plouich road not far from a railway line.

"We're going to start taking up ammunition as soon as it's dark. We can't use the road so we'll have to load it in panniers on horses and mules. Your job is to find a suitable route. It won't be easy."

I studied the map. I saw the roads, the villages, small woods, farm buildings and a railway line. It shouldn't be all that difficult to find the position I thought.

As I set off it was nearly daylight and the mist began to clear. Into view came a picture of utter desolation. Trees were only stumps, buildings heaps of rubble, the ground punctured with shell holes. It wasn't going to be easy to find a map square in this devastation. Almost panic-stricken I scanned the area several times before spotting Villers Plouich in the distance. Then I saw La Vacquerie which was almost in line with the map square. Keeping the area I had to reconnoitre uppermost, I folded the map and placed it in my map case. What a wilderness! I'd never seen anything like it (I had yet to see the Somme). But I had to move on. With my compass I took a magnetic bearing on the map square and wrote it in my field book in case I lost my way while bringing up the ammunition at night but soon I found I couldn't take a direct route as there were too many shell holes and I had to keep changing direction to find a reasonably clear path. It was going to be tricky in the dark but there was one consolation – the ground between the shell holes was firm and dry.

Eventually I reached the map square where I was met by the Major who'd come by road. We checked the site for drainage and put in small stakes where we would lay trench boards to take the ammunition. Obviously the Major had been told to keep information to a minimum so he didn't say that this was going to be our gun position or indicate that we were to make an attack. Nevertheless it seemed to me a strong possibility.

We were at the position for about fifteen minutes and were able to have a good look round. This was part of the area where the Germans had carried out a scorched-earth policy at the end of the battle of the Somme before they had finally retreated behind the Hindenberg line. They had done a thorough job, the railway line was completely demolished, there wasn't even a sleeper for us to use. A valley to the east led towards the enemy lines; on its north side a ridge ran from Villers Plouich and onwards above the hamlet of La Vacquerie; which was half-way up the slope. On the other side of the valley lay the Gonnelieu ridge on which I could see parts of the main Peronne-Gouzeaucourt-Cambrai road. Two miles away, but out of sight, the formidable Hindenberg line straddled the valley and the ridges.

Before strolling off along the road, the Major stressed the importance of finding a safe route for the horses and mules. I came back slowly trying to memorize the lie of the land but it was obvious that some of the horses and mules would fall into shell holes in the dark.

It was noon when I reached our base and by then all the guns of the Battery were effectively camouflaged and very difficult to spot. I enjoyed another meal and on the Major's instructions took three hours sleep before starting to fix up the panniers on the horses and mules. It was dark when we set off for the ammunition dump and immediately I was aware that there was considerable traffic on the road just north of us which sounded as if troops and equipment were moving up to the front. I led our convoy on horseback following the path I had selected during the morning. The horses and mules were led cautiously by drivers on foot but nevertheless some horses managed to get into shell holes and on occasion we had to reload the panniers before we could move again. I didn't stray far from my path and when I did, I managed to find it again before there was total chaos. It took hours to reach that ammunition dump. We had more trouble on the return journey and it was always with

41

the horses. The mules never got into trouble. They seemed to see or somehow sense the proximity of shell holes. We were home before daybreak and by then there was no traffic on the road north of us.

We took up ammunition on two more nights. I well remember the second trek because a horse slipped into a very big shell hole full of water and we couldn't get it out. We sent back for drag ropes and cut off the panniers leaving the shells at the bottom of the hole, but even then it took a dozen men to pull out the horse. On both nights we heard the hum of traffic going east, towards the front.

On Wednesday 19 November we were ordered to take our guns to the ammunition dumps at night fall and this time we were to go by road but when darkness fell we had great difficulty getting onto the road which was full of marching infantry, horses and vehicles. There was no doubt that there was to be an attack – with at least a division I thought. Eventually we found a space, and moved off along the road which ran parallel to the route we had taken with the shells, then after nearly a mile we turned right and reached our ammunition dump near the dismantled railway. 377 seemed to be on the extreme right of the line of attack.

I don't think we dug in our guns, but we levelled the ground under each so that we could easily switch them if necessary. It wasn't too dark and we could move about with ease. Behind us some of our men were putting the finishing touches to a makeshift battery command post, a corrugated iron hut dug in the ground. There was a telephone there with a line to HQ but only the Major and the signallers who had laid the line knew the whereabouts of the HQ.

We had no idea how many guns were on our left, nor the number of infantry ahead of us. We did know from the map that the front line trenches lay ahead less than 1,000 yards away, facing the impregnable Hindenberg line.

Our orders came through late in the evening – Zero 6.20 a.m. Our target was the far side of Gonnelieu ridge. Using a map and protractor we laid out our line of fire on the map square given. At Zero we had to fire smoke shells at four rounds per minute for five minutes, then add one hundred or two hundred yards and fire at three rounds a minute and carry on increasing the range as ordered.

About midnight we had everything in order. Now to await 6.20 a.m. Fortunately it wasn't particularly cold for November so it wasn't going to be too much of a problem to keep warm. We had brought up blankets and there were drinks. As we settled down to enjoy a welcome mug of tea we became aware of a strange noise – a rhythmic clanking noise and the sound of an engine. It was coming nearer. We turned to look back and a large dim shape loomed out of the darkness then stopped thirty yards away. We peered through the gloom. We knew that this was a tank although we'd never seen one before. Other tanks came into view lining up behind our guns.

It must be very difficult to realize just how impressive those caterpillar-tracked monsters appeared to us. The world had not then seen the massive tracked earth-moving machines that are commonplace today. We knew that tanks had been tried on the Somme and at Passchendaele but their arrival behind us was totally unexpected. Obviously we were about to go into action alongside them. Now we were certain there was to be a full scale attack and that it had been planned to take Jerry unawares, particularly as we gunners hadn't even registered our targets.

The tanks stopped their engines. An officer emerged from the nearest one and began to lay a white tape on the ground. He brought it right past our position and proceeded forward out of sight towards our infantry. This was to guide the tank to its allotted position near the front line.

Nothing happened for an hour or so; some desultory gun-fire in the distance; the occasional splutter of a machine-gun; then suddenly there were aircraft flying overhead – our aircraft. Almost at once the engines of the tanks started up and they began to move forward. We had a clear view as one passed nearby. It had a huge pile of brushwood on top which was for dumping in trenches to make crossing them easier. We saw a muzzle pointing forward and along the sides openings for other guns. We stood amazed as these moving fortresses slithered by. When this manoeuvre was accomplished the aeroplanes disappeared and silence returned. We discovered later that the aeroplanes had come over to prevent the enemy from hearing the rumble of the tanks.

We settled down to await the dawn. Suddenly at about 4.30 a.m. we heard gun-fire. The enemy seemed to be putting down a barrage three or four miles away on Havrincourt Wood. A buzz of anxious conversation broke out. We felt sure that our plans were discovered, and that the Germans would be ready for us; almost certainly they had been alerted by the noise of our planes. However at about 5.30 a.m. the firing stopped and all was calm again.

What had actually happened was that some days before, the Germans had observed exceptional activity behind our lines and their commanders had ordered a raid during which five of our men had been captured and two of these men confessed that we were to attack with tanks on 20 November. The German generals scorned this idea – they believed that at least a week's bombardment would be necessary to attack their impregnable Hindenberg defences. They were just as sceptical about the use of tanks as many of the British generals had been. Well, all except one German general who insisted that they should strafe Havrincourt Wood where the tanks were supposed to be sheltering. They were in fact about seven hours too late.

After the Germans stopped firing we had almost an hour to wait. There was an uncanny silence. I thought Zero would never come – every minute seemed like five. The first signs of dawn appeared in the sky. It would soon be 6.20 a.m. – Zero hour.

The last minute came. I counted

"Fifty-five, fifty-six, fifty-seven, fifty-eight, fifty-nine, FIRE."

A deafening crash and blinding streak of light as one thousand guns fired to the second. I didn't expect to see our shells land on

Gonnelieu ridge but they were plainly visible. These smoke shells burst into multi-coloured flames joining with thousands of others to stretch miles into the distance on our left. Then the German SOS rockets went soaring into the sky. I've never again seen anything to approach that scene.

We were on the right flank of the attack and we kept firing smoke shells along the ridge as the tanks advanced, increasing our range so as to keep them enveloped in the smoke and hidden from view of enemy gunners. That morning I was thrilled by the sight and sound of so many guns. At the time this seemed to be a wonderful experience. Little did I know what was to happen later – what was to happen on that very ground in front of us – now hidden by a pall of smoke.

Zero

Zero had come at last and the Battle of Cambrai was underway. The artillery barrage lifted deeper and deeper into the enemy lines. After firing for an hour our guns became overheated and it was then necessary to rest each one in turn. The battery artificer came along to check each resting gun. To cool it, he simply brought a bucket of water and a mop which he rammed down the barrel.

The thundering barrage went on, then half an hour later from the direction of the trenches in front of us straggling groups of men appeared. As they emerged from the haze there seemed to be something odd about their appearance – coal scuttle helmets and grey-green uniforms – they were German prisoners under escort. They came closer until they passed right by our battery position. For most of us it was the first time we had ever seen Germans. We stared at each ashen face, a picture of misery and dejection. This trickle of prisoners soon became a stream – hundreds of them passed our position.

There were many stretcher parties mostly carrying German casualties but also a few of our own wounded.

Almost right on 10.00 a.m. the order came to cease fire. We had been in continuous action for nearly four hours and

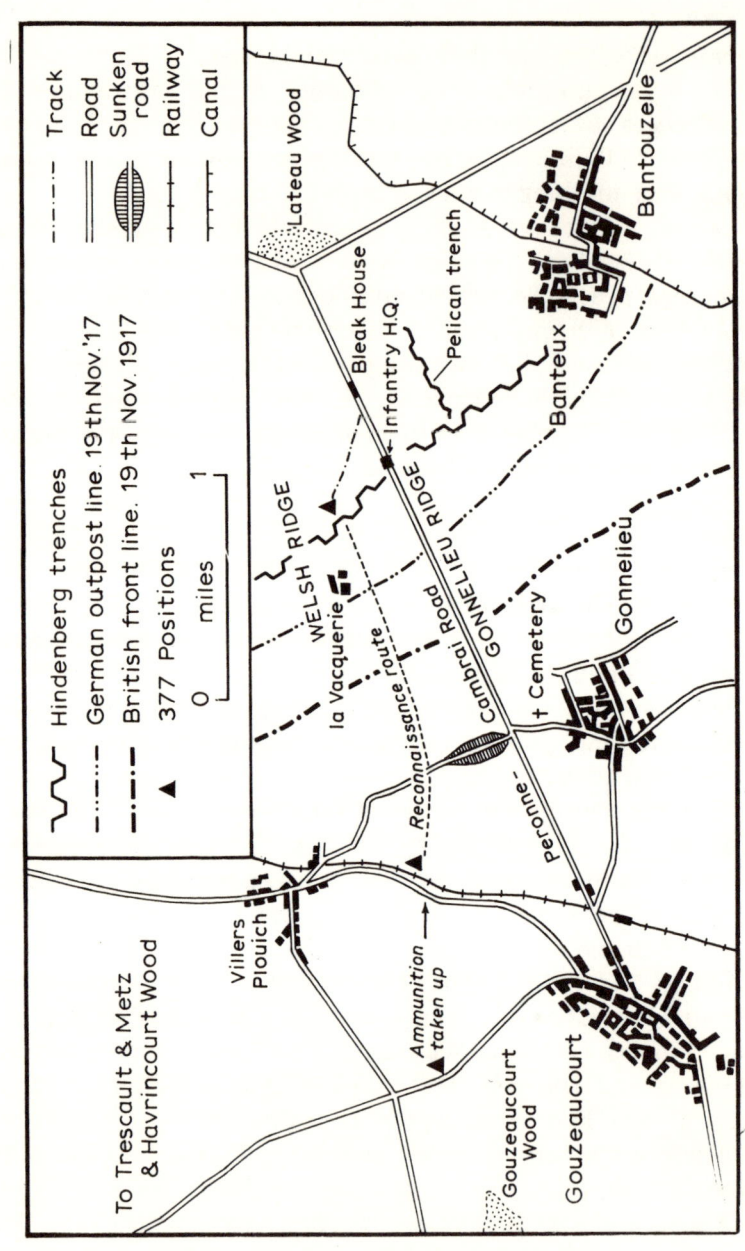

The Battle of Cambrai, 20-30 November

46

because of the extended range of our shots we were confident that the Hindenberg line had been breached. We were, however, anxious to find out in more detail what was happening out in front. Rumours reached us that all had gone well in the early stages until the tanks were held up because one of them had crashed through the bridge at Masnières. Information not very accurate as it turned out later.

At noon the Major told me to reconnoitre a forward position two miles away on the other side of the Hindenberg line. He pointed it out on the map, and through our field glasses we looked through the haze along the valley in front of us which lay between the ridge behind La Vacquerie and the road on the Gonnelieu ridge; at the far end was rising ground and, over this, the new position lay in a saucer-shaped depression at the end of another valley. The guns would have to move along the road but to reconnoitre the new position my instructions were to get there by the shortest route which was along the valley, over our trenches and the enemy trenches On arrival, I was instructed to find out the best way of getting the guns from the road to the site and then to return along the road to check its condition.

I set off along the valley following the path made by the tanks; over our trenches, through our own barbed wire and then through the wide belts of enemy wire. In squashing flat the barbed wire the tanks had done a magnificent job, cutting a clear pathway along their line of advance. You can imagine my excitement as I came nearer and nearer to the Hindenberg defences. Seeing one tank abandoned with its tail stuck in the first enemy trench, I decided to cross beside it. What an extraordinary vehicle – I reached the edge of the trench gazing at the huge caterpillar tracks – and then looked down. What I saw was ghastly – dead bodies everywhere, some half propped against the trench wall, some lying on their backs, some with their faces in the mud – their bayonet wounds too horrible to describe.

It was the first time I had seen men who had been killed in

action and the shock was beyond belief. I stared at these poor German soldiers. Never have I forgotten the look on their faces. I don't know how long I stood there. I pulled myself together and clambered across to the open land beyond. There was no escaping the horror. I saw another body and another, and then one clad in British uniform. Our early morning barrage had peppered the ground with shell holes making the going more difficult. I stopped by the body of a British officer, his Colt revolver lay by his side, a better weapon than my Webley. It seemed a pity to leave it there when it might be put to good use. I hesitated, then stooped down and made a straight exchange with my own. Picking my way through the havoc towards the main Hindenberg trenches I felt guilty about swopping revolvers but other matters soon swept the incident from my mind. As I neared the main Hindenberg trenches there were more dead, mostly ours; their greenish faces, swollen and distorted, stared up at me.

The main Hindenberg trench, much more elaborate than anything I'd seen at Armentières, was built right into the ground, an incredible feat of engineering. Using a crossing place made by a tank I made my way over and within a hundred yards reached the site for the new gun position.

On this side of the main trench there was considerable activity. I could hear officers shouting instructions and on glancing towards La Vacquerie saw a column of cavalry trotting along the hillside towards the front, a magnificent sight. On the opposite side of the valley up a gentle grassy slope lay the Peronne-Cambrai road. Some three hundred yards ahead of me was a track which led up to the road; we'd be able to use that for the guns. I went forward to have a look then returned towards the trench and took a short cut up the grassy slope to the road which I soon realized was almost blocked. Men, guns and wagons were going forward – ambulances, walking wounded and prisoners were coming back. Getting along it, through this traffic was going to be the main problem although the road itself seemed in good condition. I followed it back to the German outpost line where there was a mammoth hole, at least twenty feet wide, probably caused by a German mine. In the hole was a gun and two dead horses, wheelers, dragged in by the trace horses. This worried me; if we weren't careful we'd have the same trouble.

Back at the Battery, I found that the horses, gun limbers and ammunition limbers had already come up from the wagon line. We hooked up our guns and moved towards the road on our right. As I had already reconnoitred the route, I led the way with the left section. It took some time to force our guns into the stream of traffic, and even then we could only move slowly. After some time we came to the outpost line with its large hole. Signalling the men to halt I brought the sergeants forward to tell them to make sure that our drivers slackened the traces on the first and second pairs of horses to allow the wheelers to pull the guns around without mishap. The hazard was passed successfully and we continued on our way, eventually crossing the main Hindenberg trench. After a short distance we turned left along the track to go down to our new gun positions.

By this time there were other batteries busy taking up positions in this open saucer-shaped area. In fact it looked as though the whole of the Divisional Field Artillery had arrived.

As we unhitched our guns and unloaded the ammunition we looked around and began to realize that our new site had some disadvantages. In fact, we didn't like it at all. For one thing the batteries were dangerously close to each other, for another there was no cover anywhere. If a German plane was to come over the pilot couldn't fail to see us – a wonderful target, all those guns close together – they couldn't miss. This was the first time we'd taken up a position in the open. Unlike batteries on the Somme and at Ypres we'd had five months hidden in farm buildings and we felt particularly vulnerable.

We were dismayed by this choice of site and although we couldn't discuss the matter, I'm certain I wasn't the only one who was thinking, "Theirs not to reason why."

We finished unloading the ammunition and dispatched our

horses and limbers back to the wagon line. A drizzling rain started as we set up the guns. We learned that we were now to be attached to the Divisional Artillery and our instructions would come from the CRA (Commander Royal Artillery). We laid out our line of fire by map and compass in accordance with his orders. Our target lay in the neighbourhood of Masnières away to the north-east. We were concerned to discover that our line of fire was over another battery.

Although we didn't come into action that evening, the atmosphere was far from calm and peaceful. There was feverish activity all around us, and we could hear the continuous hum of traffic on the road, half a mile away. At dusk I noticed the cavalry which I'd seen earlier, again up on the ridge beyond La Vacquerie, but this time moving in the other direction away from the front. There was a continuous noise of distant gun-fire and as soon as night fell flashes of light lit up the sky.

Hearing that our quarters had been fixed up in the Hindenberg line near our guns, I went to investigate. The steps down were at least eighteen inches apart; I climbed to the bottom more than twenty feet below. What a wonderful place; there was a large panelled room with many small rooms and recesses off the passages. There was a proper cook house and all sorts of conveniences – a home from home.

It wasn't long before our cook produced a splendid meal which we washed down with excellent wine left behind by the Germans. It was the first time we'd eaten together since Armentières.

Later I negotiated the steep steps for a final look round outside. It was now raining heavily but my men were cheerful, equally delighted with their quarters and the provisions won from the enemy. They joked about German sausages and German wine, and someone remarked that we needn't have bothered bringing the caravan. There was some conjecture about its whereabouts – none of us had seen it since we arrived near Metz. In fact, we never saw it again.

I lingered for a while to chat with Sergeant Watson and

Sergeant Gray. They had done magnificent work since I had taken over the left section two weeks earlier. What a two weeks; we'd almost forgotten what it was like to have a night's sleep. As for today, it seemed like an age since the count-down. I'm certain we all wished we knew more about what was happening but of course we couldn't even discuss it. Our immediate thoughts were of a comfortable sleep in our new quarters. All seemed well enough for the time-being. We bid each other "Good-night" and returned to our dugouts.

Duncan had arranged my valise in one of the small rooms. We'd been on the go now for over seventy hours, and we hadn't had our clothes off since leaving Armentières. As we might be in action any minute, there was still no question of undressing, but I took off my boots. It was wonderful to get my head down.

I've never forgotten that day and I can still see the green faces of the dead.

Zero Plus One

Wednesday 21 November dawned all too soon. Duncan appeared with steaming hot water for shaving and washing. He had tried to clean my boots and he brought a fresh pair of socks. What a pleasure it was to wake up in the warmth of this extraordinary dugout, but there was no time to waste before joining Smith and Martin for breakfast. The Major had already gone up to the command post to be available for instructions from the CRA.

We tried hard not to talk about the events of the previous day. It was obvious that the British had scored a success and yet I'm certain we felt that all had not gone according to plan. For instance, why did the cavalry return from the front and surely only an unexpected setback would have caused a brass hat to deploy his artillery in such an unsuitable position as this one near La Vacquerie.

Armentières seemed a world away. We finished our breakfast quickly and donned our battle gear, the strap of a Sam Browne essential now as part of the attachment for revolver and ammunition pouch. Then there were field glasses, a map case, compass and gas mask. We climbed the steep steps to the gloomy world outside. It was still raining. We looked at the murky sky, dull and overcast, bad flying weather, just what we wanted; with a bit of luck the Germans would remain in ignorance of our vulnerable position.

We squelched through the matted grass to our guns. Not far behind, the Major sat at the telephone in the command post, another makeshift hut of corrugated iron. Sergeant Watson and Sergeant Gray, each with their three gunners, stood by the guns which had been left ready for action overnight. We settled down to await orders.

We hadn't long to wait. The Major passed on an order to fire on a target about 3,500 yards on the far side of Lateau Wood – HE two rounds a minute. We had no idea whether this was to enable our infantry to make a further advance or to protect them from a counter-attack. Our gun drill went like clockwork. I stood at the regulation place behind the two guns; each sergeant by the trail of his gun; Number Three on the left-hand seat aligned the gun on the target; Number Four loaded a shell into the breech; Number Two, on the right-hand seat, closed the breech and shouted:

"Ready."

The Sergeant gave the order:

"Fire."

Number Two pulled the lanyard. After yesterday, we could have done it in our sleep.

The regular blast of both guns continued relentlessly; roaring in unison with the divisional artillery. Suddenly, I noticed a Jerry plane. It came right over our position, made a brief circuit then quickly headed back. Without doubt he had spotted us and would relay the information to enemy Batteries.

For another half hour we went on firing without interruption. Then it started. A shell landed within a hundred yards. It was followed by another and yet another, then I heard a big one coming straight at us. As I flopped down, the gun on my left rose up on its muzzle with the trail upwards. For a moment Sergeant Watson seemed suspended in the air before he went whirling out of sight. There was a deafening crash, metal flew in all directions. I struggled to my feet. The feeling of shock was such as I had never before experienced. The mangled bodies of Sergeant Watson and his men lay within twelve yards of me — I could do nothing to aid them.

Suddenly, I was overtaken by a furious anger.

"Double the rate of fire," I shouted.

Within seconds Gray and his men were firing at top speed. Now it was no longer a military exercise. We were firing for revenge.

It was a stupid action on my part but I think it helped us all. For a few minutes the gun was blazing away, firing all out, until I recovered sufficiently to order, "Return to normal rate of fire."

The Major arrived at the smashed gun at about the same time as a stretcher party. All around us guns continued firing as we stood silent whilst the bodies were lifted onto stretchers and taken away. We made an effort to speak but the words wouldn't come. One of us mumbled something about the wrecked gun and we stood there, a couple of yards apart, pretending to examine the heap of metal.

Suddenly a large HV shell landed right between us. The rush of air threw us to the ground.

"A dud. Thank God." Martin's voice. He helped us to our feet. We were thoroughly shaken.

"I think you'd better go to the mess, I'll take command," he said.

We moved slowly to the trench, and climbed down the steps with difficulty.

Somebody poured out two stiff whiskies, which we drank in silence. There was nothing we could say. We sat by the table for about fifteen minutes before going back up the steps.

The Major returned to the command post and I to my remaining gun. I had a word with Sergeant Gray and his gunners but there was little I could do to comfort them.

It wasn't long before the order came through to cease fire and we didn't fire again that day, although the Germans continued to send over the odd shell.

When it was dark I went to the mess for a meal. I was sitting at the table trying to eat when a runner appeared.

"Sir, your other gun has been hit, one of your men is dead and Sergeant Gray is shell-shocked."

I rushed back up the steps and ran to the smashed gun. A stretcher party had already taken away the dead gunner. A medical orderly remained with Sergeant Gray who was lying on a bank of soil near the trench in a terrible state, shaking and incoherent. We spent some time talking to him trying to calm him down and comfort him, but to no avail. In the end I had to let them take him away to the dressing station.

I went to the men's dugout to find my three surviving gunners. All I could do was to see that they were as warm and comfortable as possible. I stayed there talking but I doubt whether I made sense or was of any help. We found it impossible to accept that we'd never see our friends again. We'd been such a happy community at Armentières and now the grief was shared by every man in the Battery. We were completely shattered.

Later I returned to my own dugout to rest on my valise. Duncan appeared, his face very pale. He took away my muddy and bloodstained boots.

Zero Plus Two
Next morning there was no comfort in the hot water brought by Duncan and it was an effort to climb to the top of the trench where so many familiar faces were missing and where I had no guns. I wandered around in a daze trying to make myself useful.

In the command post the Major was at the telephone. He repeated an order to fire on a new target more easterly than the one we had been given before. I watched as the guns of the centre and right sections were aligned and noticed that their lines of fire were over a divisional battery two hundred yards in front.

An hour later I was still at the command post when the CRA arrived, red-faced and furious. The Major and I stood at attention before him. One of our shells had killed a man at the battery in front. We were appalled but knowing Smith and Martin we realized it must have been an accident. The CRA raised hell, it was entirely due to our negligence and if it wasn't for the inconvenience he would have put the Major under arrest. The Major dared not tell him that it was his own fault for sighting our position so we had to fire over the Battery in front, so that any defective shell which burst prematurely might be fatal.

At noon the Major confirmed the arrangement for the burial of our dead. He couldn't leave the gun line himself but I could join the burial party with my three surviving gunners. After the ceremony I was to leave my men at the wagon line and return on my own.

We started our sad journey. We rode in the wagon with our dead, wending our way through the traffic on the main road. Near the wagon line we picked up a party of men with rifles, picks and shovels and there was a padre and a bugler. Somewhere near Gouzeaucourt Wood we dug a grave. The padre read the burial service, rifles were fired and the bugler sounded the last post.

Zero Plus Three to Zero Plus Nine

Friday came, 23 November, still no activity on our front, unlike the northern sector where from time to time it sounded as though all hell had been let loose. All day long nothing happened to us. No orders came, no information, only odd rumours from the wagon line. I can still picture the scene when darkness fell, our waiting guns and gunners silhouetted by the flashes of distant gun-fire. Because of the emphasis on secrecy there was no information. I'm convinced that we in 377 Battery didn't even known the name or number of the division to which we were attached, and we certainly didn't know the name of its commander or those above him! Years later I found out that we had been with the 12th Division commanded by Major General A.B. Scott, augmenting the 63rd Brigade.

By Zero plus four, Saturday, our SOS lines were on our flank over Gonnelieu ridge. We were given a target there and found that our fire would barely clear the crest. The weather was appalling, a mixture of snow, sleet and rain, grim conditions for the infantry who, we could only guess, were advancing under our barrage. When the action ceased all tongues were wagging – however could we support the infantry with a trajectory blocked by this ridge? If the enemy came within our front line there'd be nothing we could do, our position was pretty useless for attack and would be nothing short of disastrous in defence.

The next four days dragged on. We heard more and more rumours. The only certain information was that the attack on the enemy was now confined to the north and that our task was to consolidate the ground which had been gained. But as gunners we couldn't see what contribution we could make from that restricted place. We didn't even know for certain the whereabouts of our front line. Our maps were out of date now, only showing the situation before 20 November. We could not think why we did not move back to our first gun position where we could have given better cover to our infantry.

On a more personal level, we heard from the wagon line that Sergeant Gray had insisted on returning to duty. He was still far from well but he'd pulled himself together by sheer grit and determination.

There was no other news to cheer us. In fact, we felt more and more apprehensive. Then, at last, on Thursday 29 November, an order came through: 377 Battery was to leave the Divisional Artillery and move back to a position near Gonnelieu on the south side of the Peronne-Cambrai road. This move, we thought, should have been made days ago.

Horses and limbers were brought up and although I, personally, had no guns left, there was plenty of work to do. Everything we'd brought forward had to be re-packed; the battery "office" equipment, the paraphernalia from our messes and the stocks of unused ammunition. When we were nearly ready the Major said:

"Carlos, we must find out what's happening. I want you to act as liaison officer. Go to the Infantry Battalion Headquarters and see if you can find out the exact position of our front. I'm afraid there aren't any lines available." This meant I'd have no means of communication.

Darkness was falling as I left. I walked the half mile up the grassy slope keeping the main Hindenberg trenches on my right hand side. The HQ dugout was built under the Cambrai road in the main Hindenberg trench. There I reported to the Commanding Officer, who was, I believe, Colonel of the 9th Royal Fusiliers Infantry Battalion. I told him that I had been sent as liaison officer from 377 Battery of the 169 (Army) Brigade RFA which was taking up a position north-west of Gonnelieu, and that we needed more accurate information about infantry deployment. I added that I hadn't got a field line and he nearly exploded; an artillery liaison officer without a line, this was the last straw. He took one look at me and, realising I could hardly be held responsible for the misdeeds of Higher Command, calmed down and led me to the map. There was no real front line, the three infantry brigades of the Division (35th, 36th and 37th) were strung out in converted German communications trenches along a three-mile front.

Our division was now defending the right flank of the original attack, and its line extended from Lateau Wood south-east to a point on the northern edge of Banteux Ravine. The nearest stretch of line to his infantry HQ was only a short distance away, over the crest of Gonnelieu ridge, in Pelican trench. At no point was any part of the front line well placed for observation of the enemy trenches or the strategic St Quentin canal which lay in the valley beyond. Between the enemy front line and the canal, which was not completed before the war, and was in fact only a large ditch, lay a series of lesser ridges, small villages and wooded areas.

"Ideal cover for Jerry," commented the Colonel.

To my surprise the Colonel talked freely as if we were of equal rank, maybe it was because I was much older and he felt a need to let off stream. He described how on 20 November they had followed the tanks, overunning the Hindenberg trenches, meeting with little resistance until they reached Lateau Wood. By mid-day they had captured all the objectives allocated to them with very few casualties. It had been an overwhelming success and as far as he knew it had been the same story all along our sector. In fact the Colonel told me that a patrol from the 7th Sussex, with whom he had shared this dugout until they had moved along the road near to Bleak House, had advanced beyond their objectives on the first day and had gone down into the valley and crossed the canal, and found that the Germans had panicked and had evacuated the villages of Banteux and Batouzelle. This information had been passed back to Corps HQ but to the great disappointment of the 7th Sussex no permission to occupy was forthcoming.

Since then nothing had gone right. After three days Corps HQ had awoken to the importance of securing the position along the flank (or, as we now know had been commanded to do so by the Commander-in-Chief). An advance towards the canal which could so easily have been taken on the first day was ordered, and the infantry mounted an attack. This was Saturday, which was the day we'd had problems firing over the ridge. But by then it was too late, the Germans had returned in strength. Another attack on the Sunday also failed. There were heavy casualties on both days.

I well remember the Colonel telling me that his men were in very poor fettle – absolutely exhausted. He told me that the converted German communication trenches, now our front line trenches, provided little shelter, that they'd had difficulty providing hot food for the men and that even when they were supposed to be "in support", there was no let-up, working parties were on the go round the clock trying to make improvements. He added that relief had been promised by Corps HQ and should have arrived after three days, but ten days had elapsed and there was still no sign of it. Not only were the men exhausted and had suffered heavy casualties, but they were also defending a much extended line.

He was very worried about their situation but I am certain that at that time he had had no warning of an impending counter-attack. All he expected was relief after being in action continuously for ten days. The Colonel took me down to show me the sleeping quarters. It was an even more elaborate dugout than the one we had just vacated. We joined the Adjutant and one or two other officers for a meal. They made me very welcome and I have never forgotten their friendliness.

At about ten o'clock the Colonel and I went up to the top for a last look round. We stood behind the parapet staring out into the dark night. The weather had taken a turn for the better. The odd Very light rose in the sky; there was the occasional splutter from a distant machine-gun. Then there was silence.

"It's very quiet," I said.

"Too quiet," remarked the Colonel.

Zero Plus Ten

The Colonel woke me at a quarter to six,

"There's gun-fire," he said. "Come up on top."

I pulled on my boots, grabbed my tin hat and within a couple of minutes we were looking over the parapet. It was very dark with little to be seen, a heavy morning mist concealing gun flashes. We stood listening to a steady rumble of guns. The Colonel asked what I thought was happening.

"It could be 377 firing on SOS lines," I said.

"No," he said. "There's no activity there," indicating our trenches over the ridge.

We listened again; the noise was further south. Why further south? That area hadn't been involved in the battle up to now.

59

The Colonel was certain that there was no activity on our front nor had there been any warning of attack or counter-attack elsewhere – so what was happening?

I know now from historical accounts that further south the Commander of VII Corps, Lieutenant General Snow, had been increasingly worried by the build-up of enemy troops on his front, which had been reported, not only by his own observers, but also by Royal Flying Corps reconnaissance aircraft. He was convinced that the Germans were preparing a counter-attack. Some days earlier he had sent a warning to the neighbouring III Corps Commander, General Poultney, and to the Army Commander, General Byng, that his (Snow's) information was that such an attack might take place on the 29th or 30 at the Banteux Ravine. In view of GHQ's opinion that the enemy was too weak to mount a counter-offensive at this stage and that when one was mounted it would come from the north, the commanders did not take the warning seriously. Meanwhile, Snow had kept his divisions on the alert, particularly the 55th Division commanded by Major General Jeudwine, whose line joined our 12th Division line at the Banteux Ravine. It was this very Jeudwine who, having failed to gain cooperation from our divisional Commander, Major General Scott, had ordered his 55th Division to put down harassing fire on the German assembly positions.

Of course, we were totally unaware of these developments as we stood shivering by the parapet. The unexplained gunfire was ominous, we were certainly apprehensive.

"It's cold standing here," said the Colonel. "Let's go down and have some breakfast. I think we're in for a battle."

The cooks were roused and ordered to get breakfast as soon as possible. I remember it was a good tuck in, porridge, a large plateful of bacon, and bread and coffee. Other officers were there, obviously on the alert. After I finished breakfast, I collected my equipment and kit. As soon as I had found out what was happening it would be my duty to return to the Battery to brief the Major.

At about 7.00 a.m. I returned to the top. There was now a heavy barrage and I had no doubt about this action, German big guns were plastering our front beyond Gonnelieu. I knew this because I could hear the crump crump of the shells as they landed. But there was still no sign of SOS rockets from our trenches in the sector nearer to us. It was nearly light but thick mist still lay in the valley. The look-out was built on the La Vacquerie side of the road. On the other side communications trenches ran at right angles to the road leading over the hills to our front line. Standing by the parapet I listened to the gun-fire.

I looked along the Peronne-Cambrai road towards Gonnelieu but because of a slight rise in the road, I could only see three hundred yards ahead. Some way beyond, our men would be manning the guns. Feeling quite useless here, I had an overwhelming desire to rejoin them as soon as possible. Down below again, I consulted the Colonel who had no news except that all communications from HQ were cut; but if I waited a while it was possible that information would be brought by a runner. He was still certain that nothing was happening on our front as there had been no reports of shelling at all and no SOS. He had barely finished speaking when a runner came in with blood all over his face.

"Sir, Jerries are fighting in our trenches," he gasped.

The Colonel was dumbfounded. He could hardly believe his ears. For a moment he stood stock still. Then he issued a stream of orders. There was no panic, he had everything under control.

There were bursts of rifle fire. Dashing back to the top I saw stragglers carrying rifles appear over the hill along the communication trenches. Some passed along the trench under the road and came up to the position behind the parapet. They began to fire on one of the trenches, but I couldn't see a Jerry anywhere. By this time I had the Colt revolver in my hand feeling very scared indeed at the prospect of meeting the enemy face to face.

The noise of the guns grew louder. After a while I took out my field glasses and stepped up higher on the parapet to get a better view. There was nothing to be seen along the trenches. Then I turned to look along the road in the direction of Gonnelieu where three or four men were crossing it some two hundred yards away. There was something wrong with their appearance – by God, they were Jerries. I couldn't believe my eyes. I adjusted the glasses and looked again. There was no doubt about the coal scuttle helmets.

I felt I must tell the Colonel and then get back to the Battery immediately. I stepped down and turned round – there was the Colonel. I opened my mouth to tell him about the Jerries but he'd already seen them. In my haste I said, "Can you bring your men up to the road; I'll go back to the Battery and get them to put down a barrage on the south side?"

"That's all very well, but you can't get back to the Battery, you're cut off."

"I'll go back down the valley where I know my way," I replied.

"Well you can try."

I moved quickly to the side of the look-out. The Colonel spared a moment to follow me.

"I wish you luck – you'll need it."

As I slithered down the steps onto a heap of soil, I turned and said, "You'll need some too."

It wasn't until some time later that I realized that in my excitement I'd forgotten to call him "Sir". He was a fine officer and I would have liked to meet him again. I wish I could remember his name. He obviously thought I had no hope of survival and I didn't rate his chances very high either.

I made a quick appraisal of the situation. The Jerries were out of sight behind the higher ground. If I crossed the main Hindenberg defences and got past the wire, there was a good chance I wouldn't be seen and I could cut off the corner. I kept close to the road, cleared the trenches and the wire and turned to run down the open grassy slope. I hadn't gone more than a hundred yards when a bullet whizzed past my ear and another just missed my leg. In a flash I turned to the right, there were fifty yards to go through the crushed wire to the safety of a fire trench. Bullets peppered the ground on either side but I made it.

I hurried on but the fire trench had taken a hammering on the first day, walls had collapsed and I found myself clambering over one heap of debris after another. Maybe I would now be out of sight of the Jerries if I came up again out of the trench. I decided to try. I clambered out and set off at top speed, but this time I made barely forty yards before the bullets started to fly again. Sweat poured off me as I dashed back to the trench.

It seemed to take ages to complete the half mile to our recent gun position in the valley. I made a cautious exit at exactly the same place as I'd crossed on the first day; our old mess was within yards, in the main trench behind. I looked at the Gonnelieu ridge but there wasn't a Jerry in sight. I turned to see what was happening behind and saw the divisional batteries still in postion. Pausing only to rearrange my field glasses and gas mask, I set off. Suddenly I realized it was my duty to warn the gunners that the Jerries had broken through. Crossing the trenches again I ran back. An officer stood by one of the guns, I dashed towards him shouting, "Jerries are coming over the road. Some are over there," pointing to where they had been sniping at me. His mouth fell open, he stood as if turned to stone.

"Prepare to fire on open sight," I yelled and turned back towards the valley. There were two miles to go. This was my first and only cross-country race. I was by no means ideally clad, with heavy army boots, a tin hat on my head, a thick uniform and a miscellany of objects slung round my neck.

At least I knew the route. With no interference from the Jerries I made good time for nearly a mile. Crossing the trench where I'd seen the dead Germans, I sped on, still expecting to come under fire at any minute. My legs went faster than I ever thought possible. When I reached the Villers Plouich-Gonnelieu road I turned left. It was a hard pull up the sunken road across the Peronne-Cambrai road. The last lap was down hill. Gonnelieu came into sight. The road became more open. I knew I couldn't be far from the Battery. At last I saw the guns spread out along the right-hand side of the road.

Martin was behind his guns. I reached him panting and gasping for breath. I couldn't speak.

"What the devil's the matter?" he said.

I forced the words out.

"The Jerries have broken through – the Infantry Colonel wants us to fire on the ridge up to the main road." I rushed on to the Major in his make-shift command post. Somehow I managed to gasp out details. He said, "Go and tell 379 – they're just round the corner." I went on a short distance round the shoulder of a bank to brief Major Gillespie.

On return I found our guns which appeared to have been firing on the extreme right had swung round and were now firing on the ridge. Smith's two guns were on the right of the Battery nearest to Gonnelieu. The left-hand gun was near the road, the right-hand echeloned further back because of the trench (Gin Avenue) which ran alongside. Smith was with the right-hand gun. I joined the other one to help direct fire onto the ridge on the near side of Battalion HQ. I hoped the infantry Colonel would see our shells landing and realize I had reached the Battery safely.

We were firing three rounds a minute. Suddenly I noticed a man stuck on the wire a hundred yards in front of our gun – an infantry man retreating. I yelled, "Get out of the way."

He struggled to free himself but the harder he tried the more he became entangled. We couldn't wait, our next shell went over his head, whereupon he leaped clear of the wire leaving half his trousers behind – we could see his bare bottom as he dashed through between our guns.

As we settled down to our target, I turned round to glance at Gonnelieu, some three hundred yards away. No doubt that is where our mess would be. The buildings faced inward leaving a

Faircloth, Carter and Carr, newly commissioned, June 1917.
Right. Major William Neil Sutherland, photographed before 1917

Carr and NCOs with an 18lber, taken in February 1919. All were
with 377 Battery from July 1917. Left to right: (*standing*) the
Artificer, the Sergeant Major; (*sitting*) at Number Three position,
unknown, at Number Two position, Quarter Master; (*standing*) Sgt.
Dodd, Capt. Carr

Jacking and hauling a field-gun out of the mud, near Ypres, August 1917. *Below*. An 18lber battery in action in the open, April 1918. The nearest gun has just been fired and is seen at recoil

Ruins of Morlancourt, August 1918

British and German wounded at a dressing station, not far from Morlancourt, August 1918

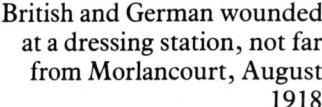

A Royal Field Artillery battery passing through a ruined village near the Somme, January 1918

A disabled tank at the opening of the Battle of Cambrai, November 1917

British Field Artillery galloping into action, 1918

Artillery horses sheltered near a ruined church on the Somme, January 1918

Result of a direct hit on an 18lber. Near Hangard, April 1918

The wrecked railway track by the Ancre, near Albert

377 Football team. *Left to right*: Lamb, McGarrie, Stapley, Hutchinson, Radford, Thornton, Harris, Sgt. Smith, Cook, Moorhouse, Lt. Gordin(?), Lt. Carr, Sgt. Gray, Tylderley

In a quiet moment before the German offensive Gardner sketched Carr and made an imaginary portrait of Carr's wife

high brick wall on the outer side with few small windows. The walls had suffered from shelling and most of the roofs were missing. Only one opening led from the road into the large village.

My eyes were on this when all of a sudden a drove of Jerries appeared. For a moment I took in the situation. I wasn't frightened but I thought the end had come. There seemed no escape. We were going to be killed.

"Stop – Look!" I yelled, turning my head so that Smith would hear. Number 2 and Number 3 leapt off their seats and without orders we all man-handled the gun to face the Jerries.

"Open sights, three hundred yards shrapnel fuse one." I ordered.

The shell landed in the midst of the Jerries but failed to explode.

"Repeat fuse nought."

I held my breath fearing the shell would burst in the gun. In fact it burst twenty yards in front of the Jerries. This was what I wanted.

"Gun fire fuse nought," I ordered.

Smith had also turned his gun and was now firing at the Jerries, many of whom lay dead and wounded on the road. The few who survived retreated to the village. It was incredible that there had been no fire on us but no doubt the Jerries hadn't expected opposition.

Soon another crowd appeared. This time we were ready; they were no match for our shrapnel. One or two survivors fled to the side taking cover in a cemetery which was on the other side of the road only fifty yards from us.

We were in urgent need of shrapnel. I helped number 4 stack the shells near the gun. Meantime the others took a shot at the Jerries in the cemetery. A huge stone cross came tumbling down.

"Sacrilege!" shouted Smith.

It was then I heared the rat-tat-tat of a machine-gun. It was firing on 379 Battery which was round the shoulder of the bank. Within a minute the bullets were rattling off our gun-shield. We closed up behind it. We survived more bursts before bullets whizzed over our heads to Martin's guns. He was still firing on the ridge leaving his flank fully exposed to the machine-gunner but I hadn't time to look round to see what happened.

I peeped over my gun-shield. There were spurts of flame coming from a window about thirty yards to the right of where the Jerries had appeared. This would be the machine-gunner. I pointed them out to number 3. We could see them through the opening in the gun shield. I ordered, "Reload with HE."

The accuracy of number 3 was extraordinary. The first round missed by a few yards, the second was a direct hit. For a minute nothing could be seen but brick dust. When it cleared there was a big gap where the spurts of flame had been.

"Reload with shrapnel. Switch back to the road," I ordered.

Within minutes, more soldiers came running out of the village. We got ready to fire. By God – the helmets – they were our men.

"Hold fast – they're ours," I yelled.

The men came running along the road and as they went past I recognized Duncan among them.

I was concerned about our lack of shrapnel shells. Only a small portion of the ammunition was normally shrapnel and I was determined to find it and bring it close to the gun within reach of number 4. I was too busy to see what was going on at the other guns but when I did look towards Martin I saw men being put on stretchers. Immediately a movement on the other side took my attention, stretcher bearers appeared down the trench (Gin Avenue) which led from 379 Battery, followed by other men – it seemed they were in retreat. I went up to my men behind the gun-shield and said.

"I'm staying with the gun. If you wish to leave you can go." No one moved.

I went out from behind the gun and the first thing I saw was Major Gillespie crawling on his belly towards me. He looked on the point of collapse, muttering something I could not understand, then crept back to the trench. I thought he was suffering from some kind of shell shock.

All was quiet now, no artillery fire and no more Jerries – only the noise of battle further off – a God-sent opportunity to prepare for the next attack. Ten minutes passed. Stragglers appeared and organized themselves in a defensive position in a trench in the bank behind us. More time passed. Then I was surprised to see Smith appear from the direction of Martin's gun.

"What the devil are you doing there?" he asked, "Gillespie ordered us to retreat."

"Retreat?"

"If you refuse to retreat Major Gillespie will put you under arrest."

"Where's the Major?" I demanded.

"He's wounded – so is Martin. You must retreat. It's an order. Remove the breech block."

Smith was my senior officer, though considerably younger, so there was no choice. I would have to obey. I was speechless. I had thought that Smith was still at his gun and like us preparing to repel the next attack. I was confident we could do it too.

Smith departed along the road leaving us to dismantle the gun. The gunners were Smith's men, not mine, but at that moment we couldn't have been more of a mind. We looked at each other and at the gun – we hadn't even a drag rope – there wasn't a hope of moving it without help, not from that muddy place.

"Take off the block," I said unhappily.

Number 2 undid the bolt. We didn't bother with any trenches, we walked across open ground to join the road further along. The block was dumped in a deep shell hole before the bank rose up on either side. It was quiet in the sunken road as we trudged along. Beyond the main road we found remnants of the Battery waiting for us. Smith had little to say. He had no

67

further information about the wounds of the Major and Martin.

Soon after, Whittaker, our seaman signaller, joined us. He had a prisoner in tow, a pathetic little chap about fourteen years old. The prisoner was white faced and shivering.

"What will I do wi' him?" Whittaker said. "I've got twa grenades, will I no' tak' oot the pin and put one in his pouch?"

I never knew whether Whittaker was serious or not but I put my hand on my revolver. "If anyone touches a hair of his head I'll put him under arrest." I said.

I felt sorry for the boy, all I wanted to do was comfort him. I patted his arm and said, "Don't worry laddie, no one's going to hurt you."

Of course he couldn't understand a word but, before we handed him over, I believe he realized that we had no intention of harming him.

We trudged back towards Gouzeaucourt Wood – a pathetic procession of weary dispirited men. Now there was an alarming sound of gun-fire coming from our left. We passed by batteries still in action. Gunners turned to look at us as we passed. We saw, or thought we saw, the scorn on their faces.

It is hard to describe our humiliation. In one place one of the batteries "borrowed" our Sergeant Major. We didn't see him again for weeks. I can still remember the feeling of shame and outrage. I just could not understand why we had abandoned our guns. I firmly believed that had we stayed we could have held the enemy.

Not for years did I learn that at least an hour before the village of Gouzeaucourt, a mile behind us, had been captured and that the enemy had taken Gonnelieu from the rear. Had we stayed we would undoubtedly have been killed. The gun-fire we could hear on our left was part of a well-planned counter-offensive from the south, which was aimed to drive a wedge through Gonnelieu on to Metz and then cut off a large part of the British Army.

After about three miles walk we reached our wagon lines.

Bell tents lined the edge of the road. We hadn't been there long when we began to feel very cold indeed and there was no extra clothing – our great coats were in Gonnelieu with the rest of our kit.

Duncan and the other batmen gave us a graphic account of what had happened in Gonnelieu. The Germans had taken them prisoner before mounting the machine-gun on the building which had been our mess. Then our men had been escorted outside, herded in a corner and covered by three men with rifles. There they had witnessed the whole affair. They had seen one or two Germans dash back after the two advances. Then a third crowd of German soldiers had arrived. To the astonishment of our men, these Germans had refused to obey their officer and despite his drawn revolver had withdrawn into the village. When our shells had hit the building, two of the Germans with the rifles had been wounded and the third had run off into the village, leaving our men to dash out to safety. Duncan had been frightened but what had upset him most was the sight of the dead and wounded lying in the road.

Darkness fell at the wagon line. We were each allocated a blanket. Smith and I retired to a bell tent but it was too cold to sleep. Troops were marching past our tents back towards the front. They were from the Guards Brigade and the Highland Division. Some of our lads were outside pacing up and down trying to keep warm. A Jock from the Highland Division shouted to them:

"Are ye the Scots Battery that's lost its guns?"

"Aye."

"We'll soon get the buggers back."

But they didn't.

4

Retreat to Bergicourt

The long winter night dragged on. Smith and I lay in the bell tent too cold and miserable to speak. I couldn't stop thinking about what had happened. I thought about the hail of bullets as I left the infantry HQ – I was nearly a gonner – and what if I hadn't turned round to look at Gonnelieu, those Jerries would have killed us, in fact they should have killed us. It was nothing short of miraculous the way the men had turned round the gun – regulars could not have done better – in fact they might have lost valuable time waiting for orders. Then if Number Three hadn't knocked out the machine-gunner, 379 would have been eliminated when retreating. Why were we forced to retreat and why should I be threatened with arrest when we'd got the situation under control?

Duncan appeared with steaming mugs of tea.

"There's snow on the ground," he said.

Another miracle – we could so easily have shot Duncan as he made his escape. I thought of the Jerries – we'd had more revenge than we wanted. It was a horrible sight those dead and dying left in the road – they hadn't fired on us – we had no quarrel with them. Then there was so much I didn't know; what had happened to the Major and Martin, what had happened to the Divisional Artillery, and to the infantry Colonel and his battalion? I relived every detail of the day just gone, it was an endless nightmare – but it wasn't a nightmare, it had happened.

Before daybreak we were ordered to move on as our site was needed for reinforcements. We were useless. Gardner assembled the Battery – what was left of it, men, horses, wagons, and limbers but no guns or ammunition. All we could do was keep out of the way. We used minor roads and went south-west a long way round to Amiens. The four batteries of 169 Brigade travelled separately. I know now that of the four battery commanders only Gillespie had survived unhurt. Every battery had suffered heavy casualties and every one of the twenty-four field-guns had been abandoned.

It was a very different journey from the one on which we'd passed on messages about a whisky-laden caravan. The horror of Cambrai filled our thoughts but, perhaps because we'd become so accustomed to secrecy, we rarely talked about what had happened, or attempted to discuss the questions – what went wrong, what might have been done, why didn't we stay and fight? We'd all lost friends in the battle, and everyone missed the Major. His batman, that stout hearted miner from the Fife coalfields, kept asking whether there was any news, but there was nothing we could tell him.

I remember very little of the week we spent on the road. I lived through the battle again and again, incident after incident. I do recall that Gardner took over as CO and that rumour got around about my reprimand and even possible court martial. The remnants of my section rallied round determined to show their loyalty. This devotion was demonstrated somewhat unexpectedly. Sergeant Gray, now in charge of our drivers and horses, by some means or other acquired for the Battery an exceptionally fine chestnut horse. It was possibly a stray from the cavalry. It certainly wasn't the kind of mount that would normally have come the way of a mere subaltern in the artillery but Gray saw to it that this splendid animal was allocated to me. The beautiful chestnut charger became my pride and joy and the envy of all who knew anything about horses.

Eventually we arrived at Poix, which is about ten miles

south-west of Amiens. Headquarters established themselves there and the batteries were dispersed to surrounding villages. We went to Bergicourt, a delightful place, up a little valley between low hills. Outwardly it appeared quite untouched by the war.

We acquired two new subalterns, both spoke fluent French. One of them, Strange, an Australian, acted as billeting officer. He was a lively fellow who found no difficulty in communicating with the locals and fixing us up with splendid accommodation. The villagers were friendly and anxious to do all they could to help. Men, horses and mules were quickly found appropriate quarters. The battery office was set up in the Mairie and this time we had a separate officers' mess in the presbytery.

The Abbé was a charming little man, always full of fun – a story-book edition of a French Abbé. He didn't seem to mind that we occupied his best parlour and I only wished I could have spoken French when he came in after dinner to enjoy our whisky.

On the second day at Bergicourt I came into the Mairie to find Smith standing by a notice board.

"Have you seen this, Carlos? Applications are wanted for an officer with a knowledge of agriculture to supervise the reclamation of devastated areas and he'll qualify for senior rank. Why don't you apply?"

We discussed the matter further; it seemed too good an opportunity to miss. I decided to submit an application, thinking that it probably wouldn't come to anything.

It took us some time to settle down at Bergicourt. We were still suffering from the ordeal of Cambrai. The trauma of losing so many of those who had made up our happy community at Rue Flourie had left its mark on us all.

We were fortunate that we knew and liked our new CO, Captain Gardner. All his service had been spent at the wagon lines and he had no trouble keeping us busy looking after the horses and transport. Horses were continuously groomed, harness was made pliable with soap and water followed by goose grease, and all wagons and limbers were cleaned, greased and polished. Sergeant Gray supervised the work in the left section helped by a young man whom I remember as Stevenson who had replaced Sergeant Watson. Every morning we were up at dawn making preparation for the battery parade. This strict routine was just what we needed to regain confidence.

After a few days Smith went off on leave, and then I saw more of our two new subalterns. Strange, the Australian, was in his late twenties and already had spent some time in France. Reeves was younger. He had come straight out from Cadet School and had had no experience of action. They proved good company and efficient officers. Strange, like many Australians, knew a good horse when he saw one. Very soon he had his eye on my chestnut charger. He was delighted when I said he could borrow him for a gallop on the plateau up on the hills.

Most of the men in the village were in the French Army and many of the Scots became friendly with the lonely wives. Strange and Reeves were also ladies' men. Strange told me that he had written to a girl friend in Paris asking her to join him in Bergicourt and Reeves told me he had made the acquaintance of Madame at the Château.

I settled down to wait for Smith's return. I still wondered whether I had heard the last of Gonnelieu and whether I would be reprimanded for staying with the gun. One day the Adjutant arrived in the Mairie to speak to me. Fearing the worst, I reported to him.

"The Colonel thought you should see this," he said and handed me a chit which read:

"To Officer Commanding 169 (Army) Brigade RFA. Regret to report Lieutenant Carr is missing believed killed. Signed X. Lieut.-Col. Commanding 9th Btn. RF".

I vividly remembered the infantry Colonel saying that I'd never get back to the gun line but I never thought for a moment that he would report me missing, believed killed.

Next day I had a much more disturbing visitor. This time a

brass hat arrived at the Mairie. He wished to interview me alone and he had brought a statement which he wished me to sign. In view of what I know now about the aftermath of the Battle of Cambrai, I have tried very hard to recall exactly what it was he wished me to confirm. As far as I can remember I was required to confirm that on the evening of the 29 November, there was a warning of an impending counter-attack at the Infantry Battalion HQ, at which I was present as liaison officer. Added to this was a statement giving the times when I had left the Infantry Battalion HQ and arrived at my battery. The times were inaccurate.

I read the document carefully. I remembered every detail of the last twenty-four hours of the battle. I'd been over them again and again in my mind.

"Sir," I said, "This statement is incorrect. I am certain there was no warning of a counter-attack." Then I gave him the exact times of my movements on 30 November.

The brass hat was disappointed. I believe he'd hoped I'd sign without question. He was polite, and said he was sure I'd made a mistake, adding that it was quite impossible for me to have arrived at Gonnelieu at the time I'd claimed, as the route was cut off by the Germans by then. As for the warning at HQ, I may have misunderstood the infantry Colonel. I read the document again.

"No, Sir, I'm sorry I can't sign it."

He spluttered out a series of arguments and questions but I wasn't going to budge. I stood my ground. It rankled that we had been ordered to abandon our guns at Gonnelieu, a terrible mistake I still thought. After that I wasn't going to be pushed around further and forced to sign a false statement. In any case, I thought I was in hot water already and another misdemeanour wouldn't make much difference.

I couldn't possible have misunderstood the situation at the Infantry HQ. After his initial exasperation about my arrival without a line, the Colonel couldn't have been more communicative. It was as if he wanted to talk – to get everything off his chest, and then on the next morning we'd been up at the parapet together in the early hours trying to account for the gun-fire. How could I be mistaken? I was certain there had been no warning. I don't know how long the interview lasted but I managed to keep an outward calm until the brass hat dismissed me with unconcealed displeasure.

After his departure it was all I could do to stop shaking. Now I could be in real trouble. There was no one to confirm my story. Gardner had been at the wagon line, Smith was now on leave and Sutherland and Martin were out of it. I could only wait and hope for the best.

Nothing came of the incident and I never found out why I was questioned, but I wonder now whether it was something to do with the reports required by the War Cabinet after the British failure to withstand the German counter-offensive on 30 November. You may think it unlikely that evidence would be required from such a junior officer as myself but after reading accounts of what happened I'm not so sure.

The newspapers had given the British public glowing accounts of our success on 20 November. At last this was a great victory. Church bells were rung in celebration – the end might be near – then quite out of the blue had come the news of the German counter-attack on the 30th. On this occasion the press had concentrated their reports on the dramatic events in our sector. It was obvious something had gone very wrong – who was responsible? An explanation was demanded. Lloyd George and his War Cabinet requested an immediate report from the General Officer commanding the British Expeditionary Force, General Haig.

Before describing this report and the ones which followed, let me give some account of what actually happened on 30 November. The Germans had assembled in ideal territory on the British side of the canal ditch, then at the last minute had thrown pontoons over the canal to enable them to bring up reserves. The first gun-fire we'd heard at the infantry HQ had indeed been Jeudwine's precautionary barrage but at 6.00

75

a.m. the Germans themselves had started with a moderate bombardment against Jeudwine's thinly held 55th Division front. It was sufficiently moderate to make the British observers dismiss it as a full-scale counter-offensive.

This bombardment had increased in intensity and then had spread along the rest of the VII Corps front.

Before daylight, at 6.45 a.m., the Germans had begun to shell Gonnelieu, Gouzeaucourt and Villers Guislain – villages in the southern part of our 12th Division sector. This was what I'd heard the second time I went up to the parapet. At the same time the full weight of three German Divisions had been launched against Jeudwine's 55th Division at Banteux ravine. Not only was it still dark but there was heavy mist, just too easy for this massive force to penetrate our line at weak points and then infiltrate our positions. After an interval yet another German force had been launched against our 12th Division front, where German troops from the force attacking the 55th had already worked their way behind some of our infantry. The infantry were trapped and, like ours in Pelican trench, didn't even have time to put up an SOS. No wonder the Germans had been able to advance and occupy Villers Guislain, Gouzeaucourt and Gonnelieu, supposedly safe areas where several HQs were established.

When daylight came low-flying aircraft had machine gunned and bombed the British troops, hampering their efforts to reorganize themselves in this totally unexpected situation. Nevertheless with few exceptions they put up stout resistance. By afternoon the main enemy on-rush had been stemmed. The Germans had failed to make the breakthrough which would have cut off a large part of the British forces.

In view of the conclusions of the enquiries which I will now describe, you may think that this is a biased account of what happened but I believe it to be a fair summary of the events as described in the official history published in 1948.

An initial report was compiled by General Byng, Commander of the Third Army. He stated that the Third Army had not been taken by surprise. The failure to hold the line was due to ill-trained Junior Officers, NCOs and men. In submitting this report to the War Cabinet, Haig attempted to soften it by explaining some of the difficulties faced by the men on the spot such as the fact that they had been in action continuously for ten days, adding that resistance in rear positions was most creditable.

Lloyd George and his War Cabinet, who were no admirers of Haig, were not satisfied. After studying further reports they called in General Smuts as an independent military authority. Obviously Smuts felt he had to support the commanders but I cannot read his report without anger.

"No one down to and including corps commanders was to blame ... the breakdown may have been due to either of two causes, first, that sub-ordinate local commanders actually in command on the scene of action lost their heads, allowing the situation to degenerate into confusion which spread to the rear and neighbouring units; or second, that the trouble was still lower down with junior officers, NCOs and men".

Smuts decided that the fault lay with junior officers, NCOs and men.

Haig was not satisfied and in January set up his own court of enquiry. This time there was a deeper probe but the emphasis was still on the lack of resistance by the troops in the British forward positions although the commander of III Corps, General Poultney, did receive a reprimand. Of particular interest to me is the choice of witnesses – only twenty-five in all. Included was a number of junior officers of the artillery, infantry and machine-gun Corps. Could I have been called as a witness if I'd signed that prepared statement?

The official history goes no further than saying that the various judgements on what went wrong were in accordance with the nature of the evidence supplied. Many believe that there was a disgraceful attempt to whitewash the commanders at the expense of the men who bore the heat of battle.

Somewhere other than the official history, I read that the slur on the troops was the most shameful episode in British military history. I find it hard to believe that there is any worse, although I am well aware that there is nearly always a scapegoat when there is a military setback.

The official history confirms that no warning of the German counter-attack was given. It attempts to record the countless acts of bravery by the British troops of all services, as do many other books, British and German. All the batteries of 169 Brigade have an honourable mention. We in 377 and 379 are given credit for the part we played in confining the Germans to Gonnelieu and halting their main thrust towards Metz through which ran the most important route up the Grand Ravine to Flesquières and on to Bourlon Wood.

Ours is only one of many gunner's tales. Nearly all the divisional guns were fired on open sights that day. Even the heavies were firing on the enemy at close quarters. I cannot begin to describe the part played by the other services. Even non-combatant units seized rifles and fought side by side with the infantry who, of course, bore the brunt of the attack.

The story of what happened to the battalion at which I'd acted as liaison officer can be read in the Public Records Office. Neatly written by the Colonel, whom I now know was Lieutenant Colonel W.V.L. van Someren, DSO, MC, the war diary records how he took up a defensive position across the Cambrai road, and then mounted a counter-attack which succeeded in pushing the enemy back two hundred yards. His troops held this position until next day, despite harassment by low-flying enemy planes and the absence of food and water. He deployed other troops, D Company, to defend Bleak House. After being surrounded these men had held out till evening, when they decided to fight their way back to Battalion HQ. Out of the hundred or more men of D Company, only one officer and thirteen other ranks reached HQ. On 1 December, the remnants of the battalion withdrew to a position in front of La Vacquerie, where they were joined by the remnants of other battalions in further resistance to the enemy.

This story of the resistance of the 9th Royal Fusiliers is by no means the most extraordinary but it is typical. How can anyone suggest that, "the trouble lay with junior officers, NCOs and men"?

Fortunately we knew little of the Army reports, nor did the British public, who still sensed that the commanders had been to blame. This disquiet continued for some time. Questions were asked in Parliament to be fobbed off with "not in the public interest" and indeed it is unlikely that anything would have been gained by a major shake up of the military command.

In fact Cambrai had been a considerable achievement and invaluable lessons had been learned – unfortunately not only by the British. There were strategic errors such as too much dependence on cavalry in unsuitable conditions, failure by Higher Command to respond to the reports of the commanders on the spot and of course lack of reserves for which the politicians themselves were responsible. The slur on the troops was an unhappy expedient. Certainly the commanders on the spot were appreciative of the stubborn resistance which resulted in halting the Germans after a few days. I know now that some days after the battle remnants of the infantry of our 12th Division marched past Major General Scott in Heudicourt, and that he called up each battalion commander in turn, and asked him to congratulate his troops.

Over the years, I have wondered why we have heard so little of the Battle of Cambrai. Many young people to whom I've spoken know nothing about it at all. They've heard of Mons, the Somme, Passchendaele, the Dardnelles, but not Cambrai and yet I believed Cambrai was the turning point of the First World War and a landmark in military history.

Churchill was well aware of its significance. Discussing the disastrous military operations of 1914-17, he writes: "I am bound to reply to the question. What else could be done? And I answer it, pointing to the Battle of Cambrai. '*This* could have been done.' "

The opening offensive was a brilliant combined operation. Tanks, having trained with the infantry, were used with deadly effect and there was absolute reliance on the unregistered shooting of the artillery, an entirely new approach which achieved complete surprise. The German counter-attack was equally well prepared. Notable was their use of low-flying aircraft to harass our infantry, and perhaps most significant of all, the new technique which added the word "infiltration" to military vocabulary.

Despite the stories that were put about at the time, and in some military histories, the British had gained ground. This then was the situation as 377 Battery recovered at Bergicourt. We had no idea what might happen next, where we would go, what we'd be called upon to do. For us the political events of the year coming to an end were of immediate consequence. This was the end of 1917 – the year of the Russian revolution. With the war in Russia concluded, the Kaiser could now concentrate the full weight of his armies on the Western Front. Indeed, by his sheer good luck some of his returning troops had been re-inforcing the Cambrai front as the battle began. The dice were heavily laden in his favour – except for one event. 1917 had also witnessed a declaration of war on Germany by the Americans; some were already in France. By summer they'd be over in sufficient numbers to make their presence felt.

The outlook was anything but rosy but there was never any question in our minds; we would win through in the end. It was just as well we didn't know what would happen in the first half of 1918. Cambrai had been an ordeal but there was worse to follow.

Smith returned, my leave at last. It was 22 December – a mess cart to Amiens – train to Boulogne – then over the channel to Folkestone and the night express from London to Stonehaven – back at Barras for Daisy's birthday on 24 December. It was wonderful to be home with my loved ones. We didn't spend much time talking about the war; they couldn't begin to understand what conditions were like in France. Out there I seemed to have been in another world.

When leave came to an end parting was hard, and after my experience as a parent in the Second World War, I realize it was even more trying for those left behind.

I returned to the battery to find Bergicourt and the surrounding countryside beautiful under a blanket of snow. The men were busy clearing footpaths and seemed much happier and healthier. The main item of news was that we had a new CO. This was Arthur Gibbs, a Captain from 379 Battery. He had just returned from a battery commanders' course, which he had attended during the Battle of Cambrai. He wasn't a complete stranger because he'd spent some time at the wagon line at Armentieres where he and Gardner had become good friends. Gardner had had very little experience with the guns and wasn't in the least upset at relinquishing command.

Gibbs had been educated at public school and Oxford. It could have been very difficult for him to follow the Major (Sutherland) who was so well liked and so at home among the Scots, but he approached the task with a certain amount of humility and the Battery gave him whole-hearted support. He was younger than either Gardner or myself; was articulate, full of ideas, and a keen sportsman. At Oxford he had been a boxing champion. He was a good administrator and a stickler for detail. We subalterns thought he overdid the 'spit and polish', but we found a sympathetic personality and enjoyed his company in the mess. We never went into action under his command as he returned to command 379, but as our two batteries fought side by side for the much of the war, we came to know him very well.

Arthur Gibbs had a brother Philip who was well known as a war correspondent. In fact he wrote the preface for Arthur's book, "The Grey Wave". In the book you will find vivid descriptions of some of the events where our experiences coincide. There are slight discrepancies in our recollections but I did note these in the margin of my copy which was published in 1920. I also made notes on one or two occurrences not mentioned in the book and these are still there to jog my memory.

Apart from the new CO I found a very different atmosphere in the Battery. The post-Cambrai gloom had been dispersed by the Christmas festivities. I was regaled with descriptions of the Christmas party, which the Colonel had attended, of a concert and of the gallons of wine consumed. Then I was brought up to date with the gossip. Many of the men had now taken the place of the absent French husbands. Strange's girl friend had arrived from Paris, and Reeves told me he was very happy with his Madame at the Château. He offered to take me to meet her. Evidently she prided herself on her English and had christened him "my little red rosy pig".

Strange told me he had been exercising my horse while I was away. At the first opportunity I took the chestnut charger up to the hills for a gallop in the snow. He was in splendid condition. I was glad to find Strange hadn't spent all his time with the Parisienne.

I'd no sooner settled down at Bergicourt when an order came for me to report to the Colonel at HQ in Poix. This was it – the reprimand at last. I remembered how kind the Colonel had been when Faircloth, Carter and I had arrived in France, and on the odd occasion when I'd ment him at Armentières. I supposed things would be very different this time.

I was ushered into the Colonel's presence. To my surprise there was no reprimand.

"Read this," he said.

I scanned the letter which he handed to me. It was from the Army, a request for my presence at interview for the land reclamation job.

"I'm sorry to hear that you are considering leaving us," the Colonel said. "We can't possibly replace you. Please think again."

He went on to say that I was an exceptional gunner – that he had recommend me for an MC for the Cambrai show – he laid it on thick. Finally he said, "Please withdraw that application."

After his kind remarks I could only agree to stay on.

I didn't know it, but it was my luck again. There were to be no ploughshares on that devastated land in 1918. The agricultural project would be no more than a cruel irony. As for me, I'd have left 169 Brigade and the close friends whose companionship was to be the one redeeming feature of the months ahead.

At Bergicourt news came through about medals which were coming our way. I believe it was Gillespie as surviving commanding officer who had sent in the recommendations. The Major (Sutherland), Smith and I, were awarded MCs and the gunners of our right section MMs. The one DSO was awarded to Lieutenant Tuckey of 379, who had rescued a fellow subaltern who had been hit by the machine-gun which our Number 3 had knocked out.

Gillespie must have known something of what our two guns achieved for although he allocated Tuckey a DSO and the Major an MC the only other medals went to Smith, myself and our gunners. When news of the medals came, I believed that he had chosen to ignore my misunderstanding of his order to retreat, and was grateful. After Cambrai he retired sick and I never met him again.

We began to make regular journeys to Poix to collect stores and new equipment. Finally we brought back the new guns. These had not been calibrated. When we pointed out that there was no open space at Bergicourt for this purpose, we were told that we would shortly move to a place where we could fire to our heart's content.

The weather was bitterly cold and I was down with 'flu when an order came through that we were to move next day. Batteries were to travel individually, and the name of our destination was to be withheld until later. Early next morning, ignoring a high temperature, I got up to take charge of the left section. There was so much excitement during the next hour that I completely forgot my influenza. The roads were icy and although I had experienced slippery roads at Barras, and had rescued horses which had fallen on ice, I'd never seen anything like going down the first hill out of Bergicourt. It was impossible to keep a foot-hold on the road. Horses just could not move without falling in a tangled heap. Imagine a team of six horses sprawling on the road mixed up with the harness and a gun running into them.

We fixed drag ropes onto the wagons and limbers. At either side of the road two men hung onto each rope struggling to keep a foot-hold in the snow. Eventually we managed to hold back the vehicles and coaxed the horses down the hill. I mounted my chestnut charger and we picked our way along icy roads leading our new guns to this unknown destination.

I can well remember my last vision of Bergicourt. It reappeared to haunt me for the rest of that miserable journey – a picture of Strange's Parisienne standing at the door of their cottage with the tears streaming down her face.

5

Back to the Line

Our journey back to the line was broken at Chuignolles, a desolate village south of the Somme. It took us four days to reach it – four days of misery. Northern France was frozen solid making progress a continuous struggle for our poor horses. We had no special horseshoes which took sharpers as we had always had at Barras during the winter and our farrier had been unsuccessful when he had tried to obtain ice nails so there was nothing for it but to slither forward as best we could. Drag ropes picks and shovels were in continuous use and any idea of a smart battery turnout soon disappeared. We couldn't even keep together. Those who could, moved on. It would have been fatal to stand about in the biting wind.

The drivers suffered most. Up on horseback they caught the full force of the icy blast. Without any orders, gunners offered to take their places so that life could be restored to frozen limbs, by stamping feet and swinging arms about.

We arrived at the first billet late in the evening – it was a group of semi derelict buildings which at least gave protection from the weather. Billeting parties had gone on ahead and there were fires to warm our food and thaw us out. I felt too ill to eat.

Next day we were caught in a blizzard. Men and horses huddled together in small groups in the whirling snow. My Old Boy stood there with his head down and tail tucked in – a picture of misery. Eventually we struggled to some temporary shelter. The men were splendid, not a word of complaint from anyone. In his book Gibbs can't praise them enough. He describes how they sang to keep their spirits up. He doesn't mention what they sang but I remember that, "The roses round the door make me love Mother more" and "Keep the home fires burning" were favourites, along with "It's a long long way to Tipperary" and also "Scots wa hae". But now there was no "Galloping Major". We still missed him and the other friends who had gone.

I kept remembering Strange's girl in the doorway. Where would she go now? Would she ever see Strange again?

The third and fourth days of that nightmare journey are for me a blank, but Gibbs describes how on the last night there were no rations because the lorries bringing food had stuck in snow drifts, and how half the Battery didn't even reach the billet till dawn. He concludes, "But at six the Battery was reported ready and not a man was late or sick." Later on he says:

"They had stood the march in some marvellous way that filled me with speechless admiration. Never a grouse about the lack of rations, or the awful cold and wet, always with a song on their lips they had paraded to time daily, looked after the horses with a care that was almost brotherly, put up with filthy billets and the extremes of discomfort with a readiness that made me proud."

Nowhere else in the book does he give greater praise to the behaviour of men under his command.

We arrived at what had been Chuignolles. Now it was a ghost village with the wind whistling and howling through the patched-up buildings. There was a prisoner-of-war camp there which housed Germans who had been captured at Cambrai.

Within a day or two we had established the usual routines. I still hadn't shaken off the 'flu and to cap it all developed raging

86

toothache. I asked Gibbs for permission to see the MO to have the offending tooth removed but he wouldn't hear of such a primitive expedient. He said he had an American friend in Rouen who was a crack dentist, I must go to him. Armed with a letter from Gibbs, I went to Rouen where his dentist friend did a first-class job. Not only did he treat the offending tooth, but insisted on attending to several others. Instead of spending a day or two in Rouen as expected, I was there for a week.

On return to Chuignolles I learned that we had received orders to calibrate our new guns at a firing range some distance away. I was particularly interested to see this area as I believed it was part of the land which I would have had to reclaim had I taken on the agricultural job.

Next day we set off with our guns. I rode in front with Gibbs who had the map. I have already explained the problem of finding a route from a map in devastated countryside. At one junction I was convinced that we were going in the wrong direction but Gibbs insisted on carrying on. Within minutes we were facing the rifles of our own infantry. Luckily they held their fire. We retraced our steps.

As for the frozen countryside, this area which had once been fertile land on the edge of the Somme, what can I say? Gibbs describes it as; "A worse hell than even Dante visited." He does not exaggerate. Here was desolation beyond belief. Worst of all bodies of men left where they had fallen, frozen in the mud. Reclamation? Who could bear to think about ploughing here amongst these men, mown down deliberately, more ruthlessly than any mountain daisy? Never as I ploughed the fields of Barras, quoting Robbie's lines, had I imagined a scene like this.

Stern Ruin's plough-share drives elate,
    Full on thy bloom,
Till crush'd beneath the furrow's weight,
    Shall be thy doom!

This was much worse than the mutilated countryside which

had so horrified me on that first day near Cambrai – much worse. I wouldn't have believed it possible. The frozen shapes were terrifying, unreal.

I think Gibbs had asked me to ride with him because I was supposed to be fairly good at reconnoitring a new position and also because he wanted to hear all about his friend in Rouen, but we were too shocked to talk. We rode on accompanied by the sound of gunners' feet, the clip clop of horses' hooves, the jingling of harness, and the creaking of gun limbers.

Eventually we found the position where we were to calibrate our guns. We spent the next week or two at Chuignolles waiting for the order to return to the line. This came in February. No one was sorry to leave that desolate waste land.

By this time we had left behind the worst of the devastation and here and there we could even see a farmer ploughing his land, a couple of oxen pulling the plough. Finally we passed through Jussy and crossed the Crozat canal. We were bound for a place about eight miles south of St Quentin. This was the village of Benay which lay near the marshes west of the river Oise. Here the British line joined the French line and our orders were to take over from a French battery to the south.

When we reached Benay I stayed back with the guns while Gibbs and Smith went forward to meet the French. The French greeted them with a great show of friendliness and showed them the famous 75mm-gun, which was a quick-firing gun, designed so that the carriage absorbed the effect of the gun's recoil. According to Gibbs and Smith the French were delighted to be moving on.

We moved our guns up in the dark and when daylight came it was obvious why the French had been so pleased to see us. We found we were at the back of a low ridge, out of sight from Jerry but shell holes and great mounds of chalky earth showed that the gun position had been bracketed recently by an enemy battery. The surrounding area was unmarked green turf so from the air we couldn't have been more conspicuous. The only redeeming feature was a deep dugout for gunners behind each

88

gun site. I remember Smith's comment.

"Not exactly comfortable living quarters but at least they're reasonably safe."

The officers slept in a similar dugout but we had a separate mess, a corrugated iron hut, which was only just big enough to take a small table and four chairs. The chalky mud proved a constant nuisance. The weather wasn't particularly wet, in fact, it was unusually dry for the time of year, but even the slightest dampness caused the beastly stuff to stick to everything, almost sucking off our boots as we moved about the site.

Well here we were back in the line and though we didn't like this dismal place we felt fortunate when we saw the conditions inherited by the British infantry in front of us. The trenches which they had taken over from the French were totally inadequate, barely in the ground, giving very little cover.

Added to these difficulties the infantry was not at all happy about changes which had been forced upon them by the Army Council in London. As an economy measure each infantry brigade had been cut by a battalion, giving its commander problems of organization, the most important of which was that in the event of a German attack there would be no fourth battalion for counter-attack. Also a new defensive system was being introduced. Continuous trenches were to be transformed into a series of mutually supporting pillboxes and strong points defended by machine-guns. In this sector the French had not only failed to dig trenches in the old style but they had done very little to introduce the new system, having put their faith in the natural defence of the wide swamps of the Oise. This was all very well but there had been exceptionally dry weather; if it continued, the swamps could become firm ground and the water channels shallow and easy to cross.

Being near the marshes there were rats everywhere and I particularly recall one ghastly outpost near Le Fere where two signallers and I were forced to remain in the open all night because whenever we took shelter, rats swarmed all over our bodies.

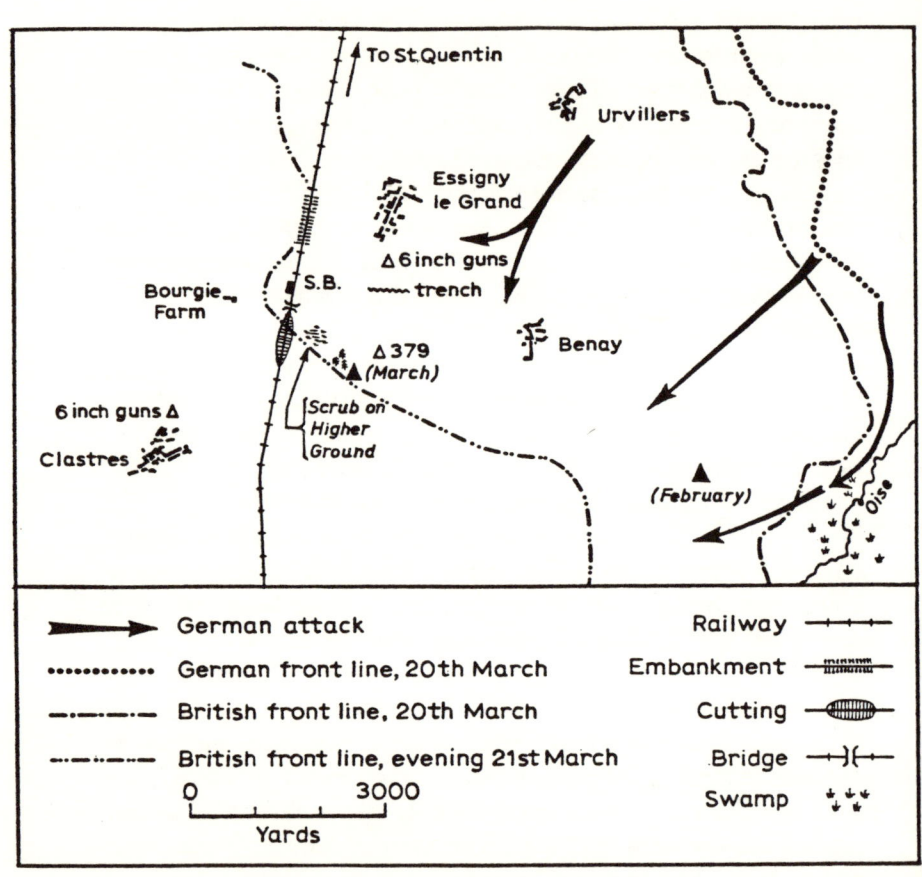

Positions south of St Quentin 30 March, 1918

Gibbs went on leave while we were near Benay and Gardner took over as CO. Gardner, the artist, and I spent several evenings together in the little hut, talking of our homes. I particularly recall Gardner telling me that there was nothing he liked better than to dress up in his frock coat and top hat on a Sunday and go to church. He was a gentleman in every sense of the word. One evening as we were sitting with our grog bowls in the candle light he said, "Sit still Carlos I'd like to draw you."

He got out some paper and pencil and in no time produced a remarkable likeness. Then he said, "I'll do an imaginary one of your wife."

I remember he wasn't pleased with the eyes and was upset when he smudged them. "There you are, I'm sorry about the eyes," he said as he handed me the drawings. Fortunately I was able to send them straight off to Scotland where Daisy had them framed. Ever since they have hung in our dining room – a treasured possession.

Gibbs returned from leave promoted to Major but he had been posted to his old battery 379 and Gardner was again our CO. Gardner had spent most of his service time at the wagon line so he turned to Smith and myself for gunnery decisions, an arrangement which suited us well. We felt we could cope. We were particularly happy to take responsibility for choosing our own gun positions – so long as we didn't have to shoulder any administrative problems. Paper work wasn't for us.

We felt very vulnerable in this position which we had taken over from the French and became increasingly apprehensive as rumours reached us that the enemy was massing to attack, but soon after Gibbs' return, Gardner told us we were about to be relieved by a divisional brigade and were to move back to a reserve position some seven thousand yards from the enemy line. In due course we handed over to the divisional gunners. Poor fellows! I have often wondered what became of them.

Our new position was a complete contrast. Our mess was located in Bourgie farm which was situated on a small hill surrounded by some trees. To reach our gun position we walked downhill along a track which led over a stone railway bridge, then turned right skirting higher ground covered in scrub.

We dug the 377 guns into a five-foot high sandy bank beside the track. We dug bivvies between the guns and covered the lot with camouflage nets, then set up the cook house in the scrub to our left. To our surprise Gibbs took up a site further forward in the open.

All the guns faced north-north-east with a wide open view up a grassy slope towards Essigny, which was more than a mile away over the ridge. The railway line, on the left of our guns, ran in a gorge through the higher ground. North of this, still in the cutting, was the bridge which we had to cross to reach Bourgie farm. One hundred yards further on, the hill flattened out and the railway then ran on an embankment where there was a signal box which couldn't be seen from the 377 guns but was in view of the 379 guns.

We seemed to be tied to 379 for we shared the same mess, sleeping quarters and battery control. Both batteries had fewer officers and men than at Armentières and Cambrai. Gibbs and Gardner slept in the battery office, while Smith, Reeves, Gibbs' three subalterns, and I slept in an adjacent room. One of Gibbs' subalterns, was called Bleazard. At least as old as me, a married man with a small son, he'd had by far the most experience of fighting in France. He was what was known in some batteries as a ranker having been promoted from a sergeant. Strictly speaking, I was a ranker too. Smith and I thought highly of Bleazard who was a mine of information and had a delightful sense of humour. Gibbs' other subalterns, were almost straight from public school, very young and inexperienced. At the wagon line, Strange was with 377 and Tuckey with 379. As for the other two batteries, 376 and 378, I believe they were somewhere to the west of the railway.

It was now early March and everyone knew that the enemy was about to attack. As preparations for defence built up we became increasingly anxious. A British six-inch battery took up a position near the top of the ridge on our side of Essigny and nine-inch guns and sixty-pounders planted themselves about three hundred yards behind Bourgie Farm. They remained quiet during daylight but blazed away after dark, shaking the farm buildings. I expect the idea was to hinder the enemy bringing up supplies in the dark. There was no reply from Jerry, doubtless he was content to take bearings on the gun flashes for future use.

Although we were well back from the front, as a precautionary measure I decided to fix up an OP in the nearest of three ash trees which were to the left of our guns. The tree branched sixteen feet up so I sent to the wagon line for a dozen pointed horseshoes to make a ladder. I remember that as soon as they arrived I started hammering them into the trunk and made my way up to twelve feet where my ascent was blocked by a nest of bees. Down I came, dismantled a shell, took out several sticks of cordite, climbed up the horseshoe ladder and rammed one or two sticks into the nest. Then I took out a match, lit it and threw it in. There was a minor explosion as slivers of burning cordite shot towards me. As I had more cordite in my pockets I came down mighty quickly. When it was safe to climb again I was surprised to find some honey, most unusual in March.

From the OP in the branches of the tree I could now see the signal box and had a much better view of the railway line on the embankment although I couldn't see the ground beyond. To my right, half way up the grassy slope towards Essigny I could also see a forty-yard stretch of uncompleted trench. To some, setting up this ash tree OP so far back from the front had seemed a bit of a lark but as it happened it saved many lives.

It was now mid March and we had no idea when the attack would come till one day Gibbs' journalist brother, Philip, arrived with the information that the date was 21 March. Somehow it was a relief to know that there wasn't much longer to wait. We only wished we knew more about what was going on – but perhaps it was just as well we didn't know that

Gough's Fifth Army had pitifully small resources because Haig, forced to choose where to place his limited reserves had felt that the need to defend the line further north was paramount. It was also just as well we didn't know that our defensive positions based on a strategy developed by the Germans was far from complete. This strategy, a defence in depth, was to consist of three zones, a Forward Zone, a Battle Zone and a Brown Line or Reserve Zone. Each zone consisted of a series of strong points or pill boxes, supported by artillery. The idea was that the Forward Zone could be evacuated if heavily attacked, and that the surviving infantry would fall back to the more intensely defended Battle Zone, while the artillery from the Forward Zone would move back behind brigades defending the Battle Zone.

It is obvious we were supporting the so called Battle Zone although I can't remember whether we called it that at the time. I do remember that on Monday, 18 March we got our orders from Brigade about what we were to do in the event of a German attack. If our front line failed to hold, our orders were to protect the second line of infantry strong points (the Battle Zone) which lay in and around Essigny. Meanwhile the gunners defending the front line (Forward Zone) would come back to take up a position behind us, while infantry stragglers would join the second line. We got a map reference and the order would be SOS 3,000. We were given the estimated time when this take-over would occur – ten o'clock in the evening of the day of the attack. There was nothing about a retreat and as for the Brown Line, as far as I know it didn't exist.

Later that evening Brigade told us that German prisoners taken on our sector had confirmed the date of the attack – it was definitely 21 March.

There was much talk in the mess about the coming battle. At night as we lay in our camp beds, Reeves, and the other two young subalterns questioned Bleazard, Smith and me, asking what we thought would happen. The Jerries would rely on gas and HE, we thought. We wouldn't come under fire straight away but without doubt Jerry had the bearings on the big guns behind Bourgie and they'd catch it from the start. If gas was used we could expect to be wearing our masks – long before ten o'clock at night when we were supposed to come into action. It was ideal weather for gas, unusually warm for the time of the year with little wind, only a thick mist which enveloped us in the morning. The gas would lie in pockets.

"And the mist?"

Smith and I remembered the mist on 30 November only too clearly, Jerry had taken us unawares, but, this time, we wouldn't be caught with our pants down, we were ready and waiting. We'd hold them at least till later in the day, the brass hats had said so. I cannot remember the joke cracked by Bleazard only that we all laughed. Underneath we were very apprehensive indeed. We lay in the candle light playing Smith's gramophone till we were ready to go to sleep. We tried hard to ignore the noise of the guns and thoughts of what lay ahead.

Tuesday and Wednesday were very busy. Ammunition, including shrapnel, was brought up and carefully stacked in recesses dug into the bank beside the guns. On Wednesday we worked flat out to finish in time. About six in the evening I returned to the mess in Bourgie farm where I found Gardner on the phone, his voice high with excitement. He finished speaking and turned to me.

"Carlos, all batteries have to dig a communication trench along the back of their guns before midnight."

I can't remember whether I said, "That's a tall order," or merely thought it.

That trench would have to be five feet deep and at least a hundred and fifty feet long. It was a tall order indeed. I rushed out of the mess back along the track over the railway bridge and on to where the men were finishing for the day. I called the sergeants on one side.

"We've had orders to dig a communication trench behind the guns before midnight," I informed them. By the look on their faces I could tell they thought it was impossible.

"If we come under shell fire it'll be invaluable," I added.

They looked dead beat, they'd been at it since dawn. I had an inspiration.

"Have you had your meal yet?"

"No, Sir."

"Well take an hour off but don't eat too much. Before you go bring me a shovel."

The orders were passed on to the men, and, before departing for their well-earned break, one of them brought me an army shovel – a wonderful tool, a cross between a spade and a shovel with a point at the business end.

It was an exceptionally warm evening for March. I cast off my tunic and my shirt, took the shovel and made a start on the trench behind one of the guns. I worked hard. By the end of the hour I had made a trench over three yards long which was five feet deep, three feet wide at the bottom and four feet wide at the top. The sergeants couldn't believe their eyes when they returned from the cook house and saw what I had done. Now there wasn't the slightest suggestion that the task was impossible. If they roped in the signallers, cooks and those coming up from the wagon line with supplies, there'd be nearly fifty men available and digging could be done in shifts. I told them to peg out the line, start digging behind each gun, and keep well clear of ammunition dumps. They set to work without delay.

Back in the mess the adjutant had arrived from HQ with further orders. We had a meal and made final arrangements for the next day.

At about ten o'clock a sergeant appeared at Bourgie farm. "We've completed the trench, Sir," he said. I thanked him and told him to tell the men how pleased I was. When the adjutant had finished with us I went out and along the track to the guns. It was bright moonlight so there was no problem about inspecting the trench. It was splendid.

As a raw recruit at Luton I had been commended for my country-bred prowess at digging. Now I knew that digging

96

could be a matter of life or death, this trench might well save some of us. I thanked the gunners for their magnificent effort and returned to Bourgie. March 21 was less than an hour away. There was nothing more we could do but listen to our heavies. Tonight there were big guns further back as well as the sixty pounders, they were putting down a thunderous barrage. The Boche must be having a rough time.

"This will upset their offensive," we said.

We went out and round the farm house to take a look. Back in the mess Smith wound up his gramophone. He put on "Caprice Venoise".

"Do you think we should undress?" asked Reeves.

I well remember Smith's reply.

"Yes, let's get into our pyjamas, we may not get into them again."

6

The Great Retreat: 21-31 March 1918

Think of the loudest clap of thunder you have ever heard, then imagine what it would be like if it continued without stopping. That was the noise which woke us at 4.40 a.m. on Thursday, 21 March. I have never before or since heard anything like it.

"She's off," shouted Bleazard.

We groped for candles and tumbled out of bed. With coats over pyjamas we rushed outside. Through a curtain of fog, flashes from the sixty pounders told us they were in action, their reports indistinguishable above the din. We turned towards the line, a fiery glow to right and left. Visibility was ten yards at the most. Gibbs and Gardner joined us. It was impossible to talk or even shout. The noise almost knocked us stupid.

Back in the farmhouse we dressed, ate a hasty breakfast, then just sat there looking at each other; whatever could it be like in the forward zone? Never in all our discussions about Jerry's offensive had we imagined a barrage of this ferocity. The infantry wouldn't stand a chance. The noise at the front must be terrifying, the rain of shells merciless. And the fog? Jerry could approach unseen and if there were as many troops as there were guns – well, heaven help us.

Through the doorway Gibbs and Gardner crouched near the phone. We waited, bracing ourselves against the continuing uproar. The whole world was exploding.

Two hours passed. The noised eased a little; Jerry would be cooling his guns. Then at 6 a.m. we heard Gibbs' excited voice:

"Order from Brigade. Man OPs at once."

Man OPs? We'd never had forward OPs in this position, we were too far back. At seven thousand yards from the front there was no need for forward OPs. But it was my turn for observation duty; I didn't stop to question.

Hastily, I donned my kit. One of the young 379 subalterns and I were soon ready. Orders were to go north along the railway line, each with two signallers and a line to keep in touch. Gibbs told us that Brigade had reported a heavy barrage of gas in Essigny and beyond. He didn't add that to send men out to non-existent observation posts in thick fog and gas was as futile an order as any he'd been called upon to give, and that we'd be lucky if we came back, but it was obvious that was what he thought. Then, unexpectedly, Gardner gave an order.

"Carlos, I want you here. Reeves, you take over."

"But it's my turn," I protested.

"No, Carlos! I'm sorry Reeves. I must have Carlos and Smith at the guns."

In retrospect, Gardner was right to keep his experienced subalterns for the guns but I have never lost a feeling of guilt about this incident. Smith and I couldn't stand the waiting any longer, we decided to go down to the guns. We walked along the track of the railway bridge. Visibility was now about one hundred yards. On our left and ahead, the guns still raged. Our men were waiting. Smith and I inspected the long trench behind the guns and shouted our appreciation. The digging was a remarkable achievement. 379 hadn't finished their trench. By now there was no doubt we'd need all possible cover and a great deal of luck as well.

We spent some time improving the camouflage, loading with HE, checking and rechecking. Smith joined the signallers at the telephone with its line to Gardner at Bourgie farm. We had a sergeant with each section. I moved from gun to gun. No orders came through. It was going to be a long wait till 10 p.m.

99

Presently, the barrage eased off again but it was still formidable. The pattern had changed, shells were coming nearer. The sun began to shine through the fog and we could see nearly two hundred yards. Five-nine shells began to land near 379 Battery and there were bigger ones going over our heads. The odd shell came in our direction but not near enough to cause trouble.

At 10 a.m. Gardner rang through to Smith. Smith came out with a megaphone and shouted:

"SOS three thousand yards, three rounds per minute."

The gunners sprang to their places as the sergeants repeated the order. I started to move to a central position behind the guns. Then I stood rigid. My God! three thousand yards! Our target for 10 o'clock at night not 10 o'clock in the morning! Where was our infantry? What had happened to the gunners in front? They were supposed to have moved behind us by the time we came into action. We'd be firing on their first position. Where were they? It was impossible. My God, it couldn't be true.

Within minutes our two batteries were in action, our fire directed on the target area. Jerry shells came nearer still. We recognized the sickly smell of gas. Masks were on in a jiffy. 379 was in trouble. Earth was flying up all round their position. I looked through my glasses. Through the showers of debris I watched men moving in their trench and there was a stretcher party. Then we were in the thick of it ourselves. Shells plastered the bankside. Soil fell back into the trench but it held. We kept on firing.

The trench was invaluable, particularly to me as I was able to move from gun to gun in comparative safety. I expected a direct hit any minute but by some miracle it never came.

About noon our guns became hot and we ceased fire. Jerry eased off at the same time. At last we could hear ourselves talking. I went to the command post where Smith had been keeping in touch with Gardner at Bourgie farm. Smith looked grim.

100

"Bleazard's dead," he said. "379 have more wounded and there's no word from their OP party. Reeves and our signallers are back but they're in a terrible state – gassed. Gardner's sent them to the Advanced Dressing station."

After a minute or two I asked, "Any news from Brigade?"

"No, there's nothing from them," he said.

I turned to the ash tree OP nearby, climbed the horseshoe ladder and perched in the leafless branches. Whittaker, one of our signallers, moved to the foot of the tree. The fog cleared slowly. I looked towards Essigny. Eventually, up the slope, the stretch of trench appeared still incomplete. There was no movement to be seen. I went on looking up the slope. It was about 2 p.m. when I saw men coming down towards the trench. Through my glasses I could see they had packs on their backs. I looked at their helmets – coal scuttles – Jerries. It wasn't possible. I looked again – they were Jerries. I shouted to Smith below.

"Jerries coming down the slope from Essigny – get ready to fire."

"We'll have to ask Brigade," he said.

He made immediate contact with Gardner, who got on to Brigade. After what seemed a very long time the reply came back.

"Brigade refuses permission to fire."

The men had now reached the trench, and even without glasses they were clearly visible. I was certain they were Jerries. I called for Whittaker to come up the tree. With his keen seaman's eyesight he'd settle the matter. I handed him my glasses as I had so often done at Rue Flourie. He looked where I pointed and immediately replied:

"Yon's Jerries, Sir."

The men began to come forward from the trench. I called down to the gun layer on the nearest gun. "Can you see the men in front of the trench."

"Yes, Sir," he replied.

"Drop an HE shell in front of them, range one thousand

yards, and we'll see what happens."

Smith came out to have a look. The shell exploded on the near side of the men and they scuttled back to the trench. None of us was in any doubt about what had to be done. Within minutes Smith had all our guns firing on open sights. He plastered that trench with HE and shrapnel at fuse 1. Jerries appeared at several places coming down the slopes from Essigny. We yelled to our NCOs.

"Pick your own targets."

Meanwhile, 379 were firing on groups of Jerries further to the right. Then a message came through from Gibbs via Gardner.

"Jerry's got a machine-gun in the signal box. Can you hit it?"

The signal box was visible from the tree OP but it was out of sight of our guns because of the scrub between them and the railway. I shouted to the gun layer at the nearest gun.

"Hit the railway bank as far left as you can see it." His shell exploded half way up the bank. I shouted "Elevate the gun to aim four feet over the railway, switch one degree left and fire."

He did just that. The signal box disappeared in brick dust. I can still see it clearly, a sight I shall never forget. What unbelievable luck!

Groups of Jerries continued to appear between Essigny and the railway. I couldn't see what was happening behind the embankment and prayed that British guns were holding out on the other side of the railway, or any minute Jerry would be on us from behind. We went on firing, picking off each group as it appeared. At last, in the late afternoon, there was no movement ahead, the Jerries had been killed, wounded or had retreated into Essigny.

It had been the German Commander's intention to capture the Crozat canal on the first day of the offensive and over the years I've often wondered why Jerry didn't bring up his own artillery, he could have fired on us from the ridge in front of Essigny and knocked us out with ease. Recently having read an account of this action in the History of the 36th (Ulster) Division, I suspect that we owe much to the Ulsters' machine-gunners who had engaged the enemy advancing on the Essigny railway station and had apparently mopped up Jerries fleeing northwards after we had hit the signal box.

As daylight faded I took a final look over the countryside. Some of our infantry had arrived from the right flank and taken up a position on the bank behind us. I slithered down the horseshoe ladder, limbs too numb to grip and staggered rather than walked towards Smith.

"Go and have a meal while everything is quiet," he said.

At Bourgie, Gibbs, white-faced and grim, told me what had happened at 379. Bleazard had died before they got him to the AD station and one of their sergeants had lost an eye. As for the rest of 379 there was still nothing from their forward OP, the young subaltern and the signallers – they were missing. Then on top of that, while Gibbs had been at the guns, all the 379 servants had taken fright and fled. He was going to put them under arrest, he said.

There was still nothing from Brigade but it was obvious the situation was serious. The gunners in the Forward Zone, amongst them those who had taken over our previous position, must have been overwhelmed in the fog. We knew some near at hand had been overrun because Gibbs told us that during the battle a very young artillery officer from the British six-inch guns up the slope on our side of Essigny had appeared in the 379 trench. This fellow had managed to escape. He had asked Gibbs to smash the six-inch guns as they were now in enemy hands and he had then asked Gibbs if he could join 379. Gibbs took him on, and immediately turned the 379 guns and gave the Jerries at the six-inch position a pounding.

The 377 servants worked flat out to provide hot food. It was fortunate for me our servants had kept their nerve for many days would pass before I ate another dinner. I couldn't imagine Duncan and the others leaving us high and dry, they were very much part of the team. On the other hand, I could understand how frightening it must have been at Bourgie, with nothing to do but wait – demoralizing in that din. I hoped Gibbs wasn't serious about putting his men under arrest. The penalty for desertion was the firing squad.

Smith appeared and I returned to the guns. Then a message from Brigade at last:

"Pack up and be ready to move by ten p.m."

Impossible! It would take Strange at least an hour to come up with the wagons and limbers. We pulled out the guns ready to hook up, then waited about with nothing to do but watch infantry stragglers who continued to arrive from the right flank, joining those who had taken up a position on the bank behind.

At about ten o'clock the limbers appeared. We hooked up, packed the ammunition and other paraphernalia. As we set out over the railway bridge there was sporadic fire. The shells coming over weren't the usual pip squeaks they were bigger – then it dawned on us – Jerry was firing our eighteen-pounders – the final insult!

Just as were ready to move off, Tuckey, who'd come up with 379 wagons, was hit in the leg. Gibbs led off trying to hold the injured Tuckey on his wounded horse. The two batteries followed behind. We turned south to Clastres but when we reached the position of the heavy guns our way was blocked. They were having a devilish time moving out. It needs at least six Clydesdales or Shire horses to move a sixty-pounder gun and even in daylight with no shell holes it is no easy manoeuvre.

There were many hold-ups as we made our way through the ruins of Clastres, then crossed the Crozat canal, now shrouded in fog. We were over before midnight. I can't remember any details, only that when we reached Jussy we were sent on to Flavy where Gardner and Gibbs conferred with Brigade, who sent us on to Cugny. By 8 a.m. we had found our new position in a field outside Cugny which turned out to be a handful of cottages lining a main street. We unhooked the guns but this time Strange directed the drivers and limbers to wait in the vicinity of some adjacent buildings with instructions to keep the horses out of sight and harnessed so that we could move on at a moment's notice. As usual the wagons were sent further back. Meanwhile, Gibbs and Gardner had established a mess in one of the cottages, with a line to Brigade.

Jerry would certainly press his advantage immediately, so it was a race against time to line up the guns. We chose the best place we could find and stacked ammunition at the ready. We worked flat out – thank goodness the ground was dry. Our preparations were barely complete at 9 a.m. when Jerry's first salvoes crashed into Flavy. We had a line to Brigade who gave targets around Clastres on the other side of the canal, but even after the mist had cleared we couldn't see our shells bursting and had to fire by map and compass.

Jerry took some time to reach the canal. Our infantry, presumably those who had collected behind us on the previous evening, put up stout resistance. All day we fired on targets on the far side of the canal indicated by them. By the time Jerry reached the canal, sappers had blown up the bridge at Jussy, and our machine-gunners were ready and waiting for him. The enemy planes, however, had no difficulty in locating our batteries. With no British machines in sight they circled overhead unhindered; we were well aware that we'd be a target within the hour. Sure enough five-nines began to arrive but mercifully they fell wide of the mark.

We were in reasonable shape despite lack of sleep, morale having improved considerably when word got around that there was a plentiful supply of food at a nearby farm, from which the owner had fled. He had left behind chickens, ducks, piglets and an old sow. Quite early on I snatched a hasty breakfast and by midday it was possible to send gunners in shifts for a substantial meal. I looked forward to a good dinner in the mess but, for one reason or another, when evening came I couldn't leave the guns so that I didn't even get a cup of tea.

By evening, Flavy had become one enormous bonfire with

huge flames shooting up to the sky. Five-nines crashed into buildings; occasionally giving us a near miss. We kept our guns in action – there was no question of packing up for the night. At all costs, Jerry had to be kept behind the canal. We took it in turns to snatch some sleep lying on the damp ground beside the shuddering guns. I had a couple of hours, much better than Thursday night when we'd had no sleep at all.

We went on firing through the night while, unknown to us, screened by a blanket of fog Jerry was crossing the canal. On our right flank infantry was making a desperate stand between us and the dried-up marshes of the Oise, and on our left Jerry, having no canal to cross, was fast approaching Ham.

We knew the worst when the order came through at 7 a.m.

"The Germans are over the canal. Retire immediately. Rendezvous at the Beaumont-Villeselve crossroads."

Orders to move were passed on quickly and within minutes drivers who had been sleeping by their harnessed horses, appeared with the limbers. We at the guns doubled the rate of fire, angry at the thought of leaving behind valuable ammunition. We kept on firing round after round but finally had to leave. We hooked up and assembled near the mess. Because there was no time to bring up wagons, everything had to be put on gun limbers. Priority was given to battery papers, maps and telephones, but I distinctly remember that at the last moment I saw Sergeant Gray and a couple of men strapping on the carcass of the old sow.

We had some trouble moving off because the street through Cugny was now chaotic with troops, lorries and horse-drawn vehicles falling back from the canal.

From the main road, we turned onto a small track which Gibbs and Gardner had found during the afternoon when they were reconnoitring the countryside back to the wagons. The track was difficult for our teams, very narrow with pot holes galore but as we listened to the din of traffic across the fields we were glad to be off the main road. We caught up our wagons just outside Beaumont.

106

At Beaumont, there was no escaping the chaos of the retreating army. Every conceivable form of transport was pouring into the small village jamming the street. Gardner left us to find HQ. He returned with alarming news – the enemy was in Ham – Ham on our flank! We could be surrounded. Gardner's orders were that from our new position at the Beaumont-Villeselve crossroads we were to fire back towards Cugny.

After fighting our way through the traffic, pleading and cajoling that we had an urgent task, we reached the position. We had some difficulty in placing our guns because the fields were planted with too many groups of trees but there wasn't time to be too particular. We did the best we could while horses took limbers to shelter nearby. 379 was only a hundred yards away, lining up at right angles to us in order to fire towards Ham.

Five-nines were dropping at random – nowhere better to hit a retreating army than at a crossroads. None came near enough to cause trouble until one landed by the limbers, killing a horse. The drivers couldn't have been more upset had they lost one of their comrades. I saw one of them with his arms round the neck of the poor dead animal tears streaming down his face.

We went on firing, trying to ignore the bursting shells. All at once, we heard the noise of aircraft. Jerry planes passed over us once, then turned and came back. Eyes turned upwards – spurts of flame from the planes, then the rat-tat-tat of machine-gun bullets ricocheting off our guns. We dived for cover behind the gun-shields – there was nowhere else to go. The planes spread out, turned and came again at tree-top height. They were so low I seized my revolver and fired upwards. Whittaker manned the Lewis gun and had a go at them, and gunners grabbed rifles. We shook with fear and fury, hurling Scottish blasphemy skywards as the planes came over again. The Lewis gun jammed. We felt so naked.

Jerry returned to base and we surveyed the damage. Incredibly, everyone in the Battery had survived; but the horses had suffered again, two were wounded. There wasn't much news to cheer us. Gibbs had established an OP in the attic of a house not far from the guns. When the mist cleared he was able to see the advancing German troops, and our infantry lying in wait for them.

Gibbs and Gardner tried to maintain a line to Brigade but it was very difficult with so much traffic about; and in any case it was doubtful whether Brigade had any useful information. We in 377 had only received a vague order to fire on Cugny with no specific targets given.

Our own battery had no observation and later on I was distressed to hear that an Irish regiment had been putting up heroic resistance in Cugny. If only we had had observation, we could have given them valuable assistance. Rumours were everywhere. One was that the French were sending reinforcements but we saw no sign of these. Another was that the French had arrived but had brought no ammunition. An item of news which proved to be correct was that our Colonel was very ill and had been taken away in an ambulance.

The enemy was closing in and at 4.30 p.m. both batteries received an order from Brigade to retreat a few miles to a position just short of Villeselve, from which we were to continue to fire on Cugny. By the time we reached this next position it was dusk, but the sky was alight because the whole of Villeselve was on fire and beyond the village we could see another great blaze where Jerry had hit some aircraft hangars. Behind us towards Cugny there were more bonfires.

Enemy shells went screaming overhead as we hurried into action. This time there was no question of a line and Gibbs sent one of his subalterns to Brigade to report and ask for orders. After a considerable lapse of time, the subaltern returned with the disturbing news that Brigade Headquarters had retired – disappeared into the blue, neither had he found any trace of our wagons.

It was for Gibbs and Gardner to decide what to do. They told us that we were going to by-pass Villeselve and rendezvous on the main road beyond. This was accomplished with some difficulty because it had started to rain and the ploughed fields we crossed were muddy. We assembled ready to move on. Gibbs and Gardner were on horseback and led the way. 379 Battery came next, then Smith and I on foot because our horses were with the wagon line wherever that was. 377 Battery brought up the rear.

We set off uphill with a wood on our right. After a while, the batteries came to a halt. Smith and I went forward to see what was happening. We found Gibbs and Gardner looking at a map. Gibbs told us that we were making for a place called Guivry; he was certain he'd heard the Adjutant mention it as a possible rendezvous. We would now turn left on to a minor road towards Buchoire.

As we turned on to the minor road we saw the burning aircraft hangars close by. It was an extraordinary sight, the huge iron struts of their roofs glowed red, skeletons against the sky. We could hear the fire crackling and spitting.

Just then we were caught in a barrage. The blast of a big shell blew Smith into a muddy hole. We hauled him to his feet. There wasn't any cover. We took those limbers and guns over the ridge as if all the devils of hell were after us.

Now we were faced with a long trek along a narrow twisting lane. This was Saturday evening. Since 4.20 on Thursday morning we'd had a couple of hours sleep lying on the ground beside our guns. However could we keep going? To make matters worse Smith and I were convinced that it wasn't the Adjutant at all but Gibbs' brother Philip who had mentioned Guivry.

I shall never forget that night. On and on we went up hill and down. Every half hour there was a halt, I well remember the first one at the top of a slight hill. Drivers and gunners flopped against the bankside while the sergeants, Smith and I attended to the horses. The horses were pathetic creatures drooping with exhaustion and in desperate need of a drink. After each halt it became more and more difficult to move on. The men did their best but some were so tired only a kick from the NCOs brought them to their feet. There were enforced stops when a bolt sheared, a strap gave way, or the wheelers – who had to work the hardest – had to be changed with another pair of horses.

Eventually we staggered down a steep hill and found ourselves on the east side of Buchoire. Guivry was still over four miles. Gibbs and Gardner decided that we should wait, while they rode on alone.

Fortunately we found a brook with clear water. We dug a way into the stream and built a small dam to make a drinking trough. We had seventy-two horses; two by two they came to take a well-earned draught. Further up the stream we also quenched our thirst.

It took at least an hour to water the horses but there was still a long wait. Men slept at the roadside and Smith and I stood side by side half asleep against a field gate. By now we were fully convinced, no doubt quite unfairly, that Gibbs had dragged us all this way in order to look for his brother. We were absolutely all in and so very hungry. Smith hadn't eaten since Friday night and I'd had nothing since Friday morning. I began to harbour a real sense of injustice that I'd missed that dinner on Friday night.

The battle zone was miles away. An eerie silence enveloped us – no gunfire – not even a distant pop pop. The rain had stopped. Cloud obscured the moon but it wasn't completely dark. The waiting convoy stretched along the road shuffling and grunting with exhaustion and unease.

Smith and I dozed, occasionally we made desultory conversation trying to keep awake. We talked of our homes, wondering whether our families knew what was happening. If they did they'd be frantic with worry. In fact, as we slumped by the gate the Sunday papers were coming off the printing presses with the headlines:

GERMANS BREAK THROUGH
OUR TROOPS RETREATING IN GOOD ORDER

At last Gibbs and Gardner returned, looking somewhat embarrassed and no wonder. In Guivry they'd found a Corps HQ of another division. This Corps had been helpful and had telephoned our Corps who told them that 169 Brigade should be at Château Baines – back near the burning hangars! After providing this information, the Corps in Guivry had given Gibbs and Gardner a splendid meal and plenty of whisky!

Can you imagine our feelings? How on earth were we going to tell the men that we had to retrace our steps? How were the men, at breaking point themselves, going to force those worn out horses up that steep hill? One thing for certain, we weren't going to tell them that Gibbs and Gardner had had a meal.

The men were wonderful – not a word of complaint from anyone. It was a task in itself to turn the horses and limbers to face the opposite direction. Fortunately, we had enough space – we couldn't have done it in the lane. While this manoeuvre was in progress, Sergeant Gray came to me.

"We're going to ditch the old sow, Sir. She's very heavy and she's beginning to smell!"

"Put her somewhere out of sight," I said.

It was a tragedy that the men hadn't had the opportunity to cook the sow. Like us they'd had no food at all and there seemed little hope of acquiring rations, certainly there would be no hot meal until we found the wagons. Somehow we made our way up that hill and back to the smoking hangars. I had never been so tired before.

As we reached Château Baines, our way was blocked by a French contingent who informed us that the French had taken over our HQ. They said there was some British artillery at a farm a mile or more further on. With much shouting and shoving we manoeuvred past the French before proceeding to this farm. It had been badly shelled. We waited while Gibbs and Gardner went inside where they found Headquarters staff on makeshift beds in a cellar. They reported to our new Colonel who, before giving orders, ticked them off for going to Guivry.

Gibbs and Gardner rejoined the batteries. There was to be no respite. Without delay we were to go into action at a crossroads which was only a short distance away. They led us to the crossroads, then selected a position for us on a wide verge at the roadside before they returned to the farmhouse.

We tried very hard but we had reached the point where will-power wasn't enough; it was impossible to align the guns because when I shone my torch onto the compass my hands shook so much I couldn't see the needle. I gave up. The only time I failed to register a target during the war. I was too tired to think but if I'd thought at all I would have been quite certain that it was the correct thing to do, despite the order. If we'd made a mistake we might have shot our own infantry, and even without that possibility, we were very short of ammunition, and couldn't have afforded to waste a shot. We lay down by the guns. It was now after 5 a.m., there were a couple of hours till daylight. It started to rain.

When daylight came one look at our position was enough. It was far too near the crossroads with too many guns in a confined area. Smith and I decided to move before it was too late. 379 also decided to move. They chose a nearby orchard but Smith and I didn't like that either and moved our guns three hundred yards away. We crossed the road, went through a farm yard, and round the buildings into a large grassy field. We set up with our backs to the buildings, aligning our guns on a wood at the bottom of the field.

Then Smith and I returned to the farm HQ to tell Gardner what we had done. We had hoped for a cup of tea but we couldn't linger because Gardner told us that he had just been informed that the Boche was in the wood at the bottom of the field we'd just occupied. This time our luck was in. As we raced through the traffic, panic stricken at the thought of meeting Jerry with so few shells at our disposal, we overtook one of our sergeants directing an ammunition wagon into the yard of the farm where our guns lay. The wagon belonged to a retreating brigade which had lost its guns. In no time we had piles of shells beside each gun.

There was a straw stack immediately behind our guns. With some difficulty I climbed to the top. The large field sloped down to the wood three or four hundred yards away. The field was surrounded by trees and a low hedge; here and there gaps were made good with post and rail fencing. I kept my glasses trained on the wood at the far end but couldn't see anything.

All around there was plenty of evidence that the enemy was on the move. Balloons rose in the sky, shells dropped on the crossroads while enemy planes soared overhead. We were lucky to escape attention.

I turned to look in the other direction. To my amazement a troop of cavalry was approaching brandishing sabres – a magnificent spectacle – but whatever did they think they were doing? On they went down the field, two hundred yards to go. Horrified I saw men topple out of their saddles, horses stumble and roll over. The sound of machine-guns and rifles came crackling up the field as more riders and horses fell. My God, there were no riders left.

Jerries with rifles appeared from the wood. We all saw them coming through the hedge. I slid down the stack, yelling "Fire on open sights."

The words were scarcely out of my mouth when a messenger from Gardner came round the buildings.

"Retire at once. You are about to be surrounded."

Our limbers were hidden in the buildings. It would take a few minutes to bring them round. Outraged at what Jerry had done to the cavalry, Smith and I weren't going to retire without firing a shot. We weren't going to miss this "open sight" target.

Our gunners excelled themselves – they loaded and reloaded those guns at incredible speed. I could see Jerry casualties on the grass in front of the hedge. Others retreated. We fired into the wood. The limbers appeared. It was infuriating to leave behind those piles of ammunition but we had no alternative.

We hooked up and left.

Gardner and his signallers joined us before we forced our way on to the road. It was chaotic with every conceivable form of traffic coming back from the front, and French infantry, gunners and transport arriving "to take over the line".

Before leaving the HQ Gardner had received his orders: the Brigade was to move south and rendezvous – near Buchoire. I remember little detail of our next gun site. In fact, the following days are blurred in memory – hunger, lack of sleep – mental and physical tiredness so extreme as to beggar description; yet certain incidents remain with remarkable clarity.

We didn't come into action until the morning, enabling me to sleep for three hours. By now any sleep was an event. There was still nothing to eat. Men foraged in empty houses sometimes finding a few scraps. Hunger became a gnawing pain. We became increasingly anxious about Gibbs and 379 Battery who had failed to arrive at Buchoire. We knew they had had difficulty coming out of the orchard and that they'd suffered casualties, but nevertheless we had expected to see them by this time.

All around us the disarray of an army in retreat, but we were not beaten – not yet.

The Hun continued to advance. From Buchoire we were given map targets, and I remember I thought I might be able to set up an observation post in order to direct fire more accurately. I went forward with two signallers, trying to lay a line through the confusion of advancing and retreating infantry. At one place we were delayed by a mounted NCO. He was weighed down by heavy sacks; one of these had a large hole. Through it we saw a labelled tin – maconochie. He had tins and tins of maconochie. With my hand on my revolver, I said:

"I order you to hand over a tin of maconochie. We haven't eaten for three days."

The NCO must have seen the expression on my face.

Without hesitation he gave us a $1\frac{1}{2}$ lb. tin of maconochie – stew and vegetables remembered with revulsion by many a Tommy but because of this incident by me with gratitude. We opened the tin with a jack knife and dug in with our fingers – one of the best meals of my life.

It proved too difficult to lay a line. We returned to the guns, and continued to fire by map. We didn't stay long near Buchoire before retreating further south. We began to lose all count of time. No sleep, no food, but always uppermost the need to fight off the Hun. He gave us little respite and we came into "action rear" more than once. We stopped for a rest outside Crisolles. Smith and I, painfully hungry, decided that, like the men, we'd make a sortie into the town to forage for food. It was dusk as we wandered along the main street. We searched two houses without success. In the third, Smith was the first to see a half-full bottle of wine on the kitchen table. He grabbed it and drank the lot before collapsing on an easy chair. I gave him a minute or two before trying to rouse him. He was dead to the world. All at once his batman burst in.

"Jerry's here. He's setting fire to the houses at the end of the street."

We shouted at Smith, and seized him by both arms trying to shake him awake. Nothing happened. We'd either have to carry him or leave him behind. Then, by the door, I saw a bucket of water. Within seconds I was pouring it down the back of Smith's neck. He opened his eyes but he was only half conscious. We dragged him into the street. Flames shot from houses only yards away. We reached the Battery to find Gardner distraught at having made the decision to leave us behind. A short distance from Crisolles we turned our guns to support our retreating infantry.

In the early morning we moved west through Bussy and turned our guns yet again. To our relief, we were rejoined by 379 Battery; we'd given them up for lost days ago. But there wasn't time to find out what had happened. Hand-to-hand fighting between British and German infantries developed in

Bussy and we were ordered to put down a curtain of fire on the far side of the village. Our observation officer could see the enemy there, advancing in droves. All four batteries of 169 Brigade were in action and we were able to inflict enormous casualties. If only we'd been able to give the infantry this kind of support from the beginning of the retreat things might have been different.

We fired for a few hours before receiving the order to move on. There was so much traffic we only progressed a few yards at a time. Not that we were in any condition to go faster. It was a week since we'd eaten properly or had had more than three hours sleep at a stretch, we hadn't had a wash and we'd never had our boots off. There had been no let-up, we had been either in action or on the move. Gaunt, hollow eyed, unshaven and filthy, we stumbled along the road.

To the north, unknown to us, Jerry was sweeping forward over the old battlefields of the Somme. We could hear him to the south-east in Noyon and from where we were, he was little more than a mile away. The Brigade was to rendezvous in a large field near Cuy and there await orders. We reached the field to find an angled gateway so it should have been easy to move guns and limbers off the narrow road. Alas, the field was boggy. Wagons ploughed in axle deep. Imagine the chaos as horses, pulling limbers, were detached to assist those pulling the heavier wagons to reach drier ground further up. All four Batteries of 160 Brigade were to rendezvous here and, although our arrival was staggered, when we'd all assembled there were twenty-four guns and 174 horses – less the ones we had lost.

We led our poor horses to a stream to quench their thirst; there was no forage. Like us they were starving; hopefully the pangs of hunger had ceased and, like us, they no longer craved food – only water. Then word was passed round that the Brigade was to be relieved. We were to be taken out of the line. The news didn't cheer us for we felt that we had left too much unfinished business with the Hun. We huddled in groups, eyes half shut, unable to make coherent speech, shivering in the

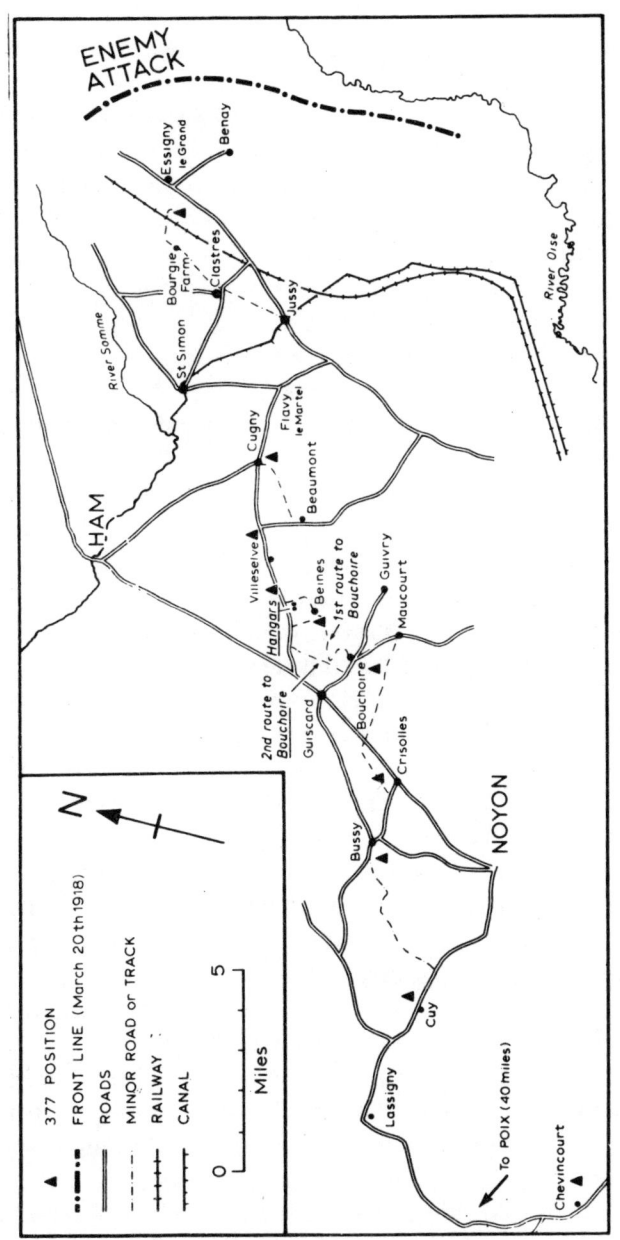

Route of 377 Battery during the Great Retreat

117

cold. Occasionally, there was a distant cry; we stirred in alarm, mustered a croaked laugh, or muttered a curse.

Then shouts – orders – the Adjutant had arrived – move on.

We staggered to our feet; it was going to be a devil of a job getting out of that field. This time the gateway angled in the wrong direction, not only would it be necessary to re-cross the boggy ground but we'd have to remove 12 yards of hedge and bridge the adjacent ditch in order to take the vehicles on to the narrow road. I wondered whether we could manage it with men and horses so exhausted. Then a word from Gardner.

"The Adjutant tells me that the Major's back. He's at HQ now – Major Sutherland is back." The news went round 377 like wild fire.

"The Major's back – he's ah richt – he's coming back."

It was miraculous, men were on their feet, horses mounted, shovels seized and a start made to hack down the hedge. The ditch was filled with clods of earth, brushwood – anything we could find. I seized a shovel myself – glad to be doing something. We were the first battery out of the field.

Our destination was Chevrincourt, far south of Cuy – out of the battle zone. The road was as chaotic as ever. We moved slowly, our pace set by the vehicles ahead. At Lassigny, we turned south. At last we were clear of the traffic but we and our horses were so worn out we couldn't move any faster. It was so cold it was agony to stop but we couldn't keep going without a frequent halt when gunners lay down by the side of the road and drivers slumped in the saddle. Every now and then gunners and drivers changed places.

Gardner was so tired he had to be held on a limber by an NCO. I had Old Boy, my chestnut charger, but I could only ride a short distance without falling asleep, when I was forced to dismount. Eventually, I found it difficult to get up in the saddle but Old Boy seemed to understand. He almost stooped to the ground to let me on his back. We straggled forward in a daze, so exhausted that it became impossible to tell whether we were halted or on the move. When daylight dawned on Friday

29 March, we really were in a shocking plight. Horses staggered along the short distance between halts. Drivers were asleep on their mounts, gunners were flat out on wagons or limbers. Why no one fell off and got left behind, hurt or killed I shall never know. At last a shout.

"Chevrincourt – Chevrincourt."

I'm told it was 9 a.m. Our "march" from Cuy had lasted sixteen hours.

I don't know what happened to the others. I just managed to dismount and crawl through a hedge before collapsing on the ground. Someone mentioned tea but I couldn't raise my head. I awoke at 4.30 p.m. Duncan had wrapped me in a blanket. After drinking tea and eating a little food, I lay down and slept again till Sunday. This time I felt born anew. Someone told me it was Sunday – 31 March.

31 March? The previous day had been my birthday. I was 34 years old.

7

On the Defensive

Our stay in Chevrincourt was short. Troops were urgently required for the defence of Amiens. Its fall would almost certainly prove an irretrievable disaster by letting the enemy through to the coast and the channel ports. There was to be a full scale regrouping of forces; depleted units would join together to make up battalions or brigades. Even as we slept the 169 Brigade guns were taken away and put into action by a brigade who had lost theirs in the retreat, and there was talk of one of our batteries joining that brigade to bring it up to strength.

Our orders were to set off for Poix near Amiens, but the pitiful condition of our horses delayed our departure. I couldn't believe my eyes when I visited the lines and saw the full extent of the horses' suffering. After the removal of days of mud and grime, there was nothing left but skin and bone. Even muscle tissue had worn away. Recovery would take weeks – even months. And now they were to be forced back onto the road for another long march. Poix was about forty miles away. Forage was so desperately short that drivers went out to buy hay with their own money but local farmers were deaf to their pleas.

Officers and men were now also clean and groomed, and we felt almost back to normal. We had been incredibly lucky. Unlike other batteries we had no dead, wounded or missing to mourn. We took the opportunity to send home letters or field service postcards to ease the anxiety of our loved ones. We saw our retreat as a setback rather than a defeat, feeling neither disgraced nor humiliated. We seldom talked about past actions only about that might happen next.

Much later we learned of the incredible odds – of the enemy's forty-five divisions launched against our fifteen. We learned how the Hun had made meticulous preparations, including the development of the infiltration techniques he had used against us at Cambrai. We learned how our machine-gunners, hampered by the fog had found it almost impossible to defend the redoubts. Of course there were scapegoats, and this time the blame fell mainly on the shoulders of General Gough, who had been dismissed even before we arrived in Chevrincourt. We must have felt very strongly about his unjust treatment for unlike the other generals under whom I served, I have never forgotten his name, and if at any time during the last sixty years you had asked me "What did you do in the First World War?", I would have replied with pride "I was in Gough's army during the Great Retreat."

At Chevrincourt, we had expected the Major to resume command of 377 but this never occurred because the "new" Colonel departed, leaving Sutherland in temporary command of the Brigade.

Our march to Poix took three days. We soon discovered, that like the horses, we were anything but fit. Already weary and despondent, we were even more depressed by the presence on the road of French civilians fleeing south with farm carts, hand carts and perambulators all piled high with household goods. There were old men, women and young girls, some carried babies, some dragged small children by the hand, and many staggered under bundles of clothing. They pulled their cattle along by ropes tied to their horns. It was the most pitiful sight imaginable. We were further upset by their attitude to us. They made no secret of the fact that they believed we were running away and had let them down. They even spat at us.

We were worn out but this journey was nothing to what we

had endured from Essigny to Chevrincourt. Reunited with the wagon line, we had Strange, the Australian, acting as billeting officer. True to form, he saw that for each night halt there was some sort of roof over our heads. In fact, on the second night he excelled himself by fixing us up in a deserted château. I was allocated a magnificent four poster bed but alas it was so soft and comfortable I couldn't sleep. I just lay there going over in my mind what had happened since Jerry woke us with that deafening barrage on 21 March.

By this time, Strange wasn't the only Australian with the Battery. During the retreat, the wagon line had acquired an Australian sergeant major, a tall hefty fellow, like Strange full of energy and enterprise.

At last, we arrived in Poix to hear that once again our billets would be in Bergicourt. When we arrived in the little village there was much excitement. Here there was no resentment by the French. On the contrary, the inhabitants were delighted to see us again. In particular, I remember one woman waving from an upstairs window. She leaned out, stripped to the waist: there was no mistaking her welcome! But, unlike the respite after Cambrai, this time there was no opportunity for frivolities. Within four days we had collected six new guns, and all the essential stores we could find.

We rejoined the other batteries of 169 Brigade and left for the area to the south of Villers Bretonneux, a town on high ground which allowed observation of Amiens to the west, and over the valley of the Somme to the north. To the south, four miles distant, lay Hangard Wood; Hangard village was more than a mile beyond on the banks of the River Luce, a tributary of the Avre. To block the enemy advance, it was absolutely vital to hold the fifteen miles between the Somme and the Avre.

By the time we reached this front, Villers Bretonneux itself was being defended by the Australians, the Hangard Wood area by remnants of the 14th and 18th Divisions and an Australian battalion, and the area furthest south between the Luce and the Avre, which included Hangard village, by the French.

However, there appeared to be no fixed boundaries, troops were being rushed from one area to another as required. During the last few days, and in particular on 4 April, there had been fierce attacks and counter-attacks over this ground. The Hun was making a desperate effort to breakthrough.

When we arrived on 9 April there was such a mix up amongst French troops that we couldn't find our position. Eventually, we were attached to an Australian battalion. We came into action at once, firing at long range, about four thousand yards, on a target beyond Hangard village. We went on firing all day and through the night. The weather was atrocious.

Almost continually large shells went rumbling over our heads into Amiens.

On the 10th, we were moved to a location behind a crest near Gentelles. From there, we continued to fire on the target beyond Hangard until we were so worn out with lack of sleep we had to stop for a few hours. Then once again, we resumed firing and continued all through the night.

On the 11th, some senior brass hat ordered us to take up a position much nearer our target on the forward slope beyond Gentelles in full view of the Hun. Gibbs and the CO of 378, who was a regular army officer, went forward to inspect and were appalled at the idea of moving to such a dangerous place, one, which they thought offered little or no further advantage as regards gunnery. They sent back their report urging that we stay put. It was rejected.

We moved during the late afternoon of 11th, joining the main Amiens-Hangard road to the south-east. We passed newly dug graves, dead horses, and other litter of war. There were no fences but some posts here and there resembling snow posts on a mountain road in Scotland. Shell holes were everywhere. 378 led the way. They took up a position about a mile down the slope on the left-hand side of the road. We turned off into a field to the right of the road some twenty yards behind 378. 379 went further into the same field just round a knoll on our right, taking the place of another battery which had been in action there.

There had been heavy rain during the day but the ground was much drier than it had appeared from the road so it was quite easy to dig in our guns. Not far ahead we noted the ruined village of Domart. Hangard a mile beyond lay hidden in the murky gloom. We registered our guns on an object in front, planted our aiming posts, and set gun sights at zero in front of the infantry in Hangard. At the same time others dug bivvies four feet square and five feet deep. Each was covered with a tarpaulin. Gardner suggested that I should dig a hole for the mess. With help, I dug a hole five and a half feet deep, the size of a small room, and covered it too with a tarpaulin. In it we set up the office with a line to Brigade HQ near Gentelles where Sutherland was still in command. Finally, we ate some kind of meal, and as there had been no further orders the men crowded into their bivvies hopeful of a few hours' sleep. Gardner, Smith and I lay down in the mess. We were worn out.

April 12 1918: It was the telephone that woke me – Sutherland's voice.

"SOS three thousand yards three rounds a minute. The Boche are attacking!"

"SOS," I shouted.

Smith and Gardner were dead to the world. I shouted again.

"SOS three thousand yards, three rounds a minute."

They groaned. I lit a candle – 4 a.m. As usual no need to dress, we'd been sleeping fully clothed. Equipment to hand; I heaved myself from the mess into the dark. In the distance the noise of battle; nearby, no one stirred. My voice rang out:

"SOS three thousand yards, three rounds a minute."

The Australian sergeant appeared rubbing his eyes.

"Everyone is dead beat, Sir."

"SOS three thousand yards, three rounds a minute," I repeated automatically. "Get them up."

Movement started at 378 battery. At 377 Sergeant Stevenson joined us. Within minutes he and the Australian had everyone up. Smith took command of the right section, the Australian took the centre and I had the left. I had four men on each gun, Sergeant Stevenson in charge of one, a corporal in charge of the other. Gardner, with a signaller, stayed in the mess by the telephone.

Five o'clock came, then six o'clock, the darkness receded. Time to rest the guns. At 377 we stopped the left section first. It was dry and clear, there was even sunshine, a much better day than of late. But that wasn't good news for us. Beyond Hangard an enemy balloon rose in the sky. I raised my glasses; there were two figures in the basket, the balloon officer – and, almost certainly, an artillery observation officer. My blood froze. Flashes from our brigade would attract immediate attention. They would have their heavies on our position with absolute accuracy. We could not survive. I tried to imagine what I would do were our positions reversed.

"What's this – eighteen-pounder batteries – one either side of the road from Amiens – two more four thousand metres over the field. Get my battery. I'll give the map square of the one on the left of the road and get the other with a switch to the right. 'Hallo Klaus! Map square eight, six, four. Fire when ready."

There wasn't much comfort in that. We'd have about an hour while they registered their targets. I went to the mess to warn Gardner.

The left section was still resting. I called to Sergeant Stevenson and the Corporal:

"Dig a funk hole at the end of the trail of your gun, make it about four feet deep, wide enough for the four of you and with a step to get out quickly."

I dug my own hole deeper with three steps up. I could stand upright and would only have to bend my head to avoid splinters from large shells. They would be heard coming soon enough to warn the gunners.

Thankful for the sandy soil, we completed the digging quickly.

"When you hear me shout 'Cover', jump into your hole and

125

keep your heads down. When I shout 'All Clear', back to the guns."

We started firing again. Suddenly there was activity behind us. I turned in time to see a French 75-mm. battery come galloping down the road. They came to a halt with a flourish, then left the road and took up a good position beyond 378. In fact, I'd been surprised that 378 hadn't occupied the place for it was the only good position – a natural hollow screened by a bank with a hedge. The French didn't bother to lay out a line of fire but commenced gun fire at an unbelievable rate. Splendid.

"This will make the Boche sit up," we said.

Greatly cheered by this show of solidarity, we resumed firing. It wasn't long before I heard a shell with our names on.

"Cover!" I shouted.

The gunners dived into the holes. The shell, a really big one, fell short.

"All clear!"

The gunners resumed action. I could imagine Fritz in the balloon.

"Ah good – line all right, ten metres short add twenty."

Sure enough a few minutes respite, then I heard another shell.

"Cover."

The ground behind exploded showering us with debris.

"All clear."

Fritz had us bracketed, he was enjoying himself; by now he'd have been on to Brigade.

"That you, Sir? I'm up in the balloon – there's a whole Field Artillery Brigade, splendid target. I'm registering 'A' Battery's guns but I want at least another five point nine battery and field-guns may be within range."

The French continued to blaze away. Fritz must have seen them. But try 378 first. I imagined his order.

"Switch one degree 20 minutes right, drop forty and fire both guns."

126

My guess was right, the next shell sent one of the 378 guns up in the air. Again I could hear Fritz.

"Wonderful, you've got a gun. Continue to fire, you'll get the French seventy-seven by dropping sixty."

But the French had seen enough. They didn't wait for the shells to arrive, they upped trails, hooked on and scampered up the road as fast as they had come. They escaped without a casualty. We were disgusted.

"Of all the ... cowards," we said. But it would have been better had we followed their example.

Fritz had us at his mercy. There was nothing we could do as he brought in a heavy battery and field-guns to hammer the Brigade. He went for each of us in turn, 379 then 376 but we could only hear the explosions and see the soil erupting, we couldn't see what had happened to them. Then it was the turn of 378 again – a salvo this time. I saw another of their guns take a direct hit. Presently, a shell seemed to have the name of our section on it but it went to the right and hit one of Smith's guns. Shells continued to land round all four batteries. 378 was in serious trouble. They had ceased fire. Some time passed then I saw George Harvey, one of their officers, come out with a megaphone. Regardless of danger, he stood at the regulation place behind their two remaining guns. Between explosions I could hear his voice encouraging his men, doing his utmost to resume action.

For the first time Gardner left the telephone and came out to see what was happening. I climbed out of my funk hole and we were standing two yards apart when I heard a particularly big shell coming our way.

"Cover."

The shell was going left, I saw Harvey go down before I fell to the ground. Within seconds Gardner was beside me clutching his chest. We got a stretcher and carried him to the mess. He was still conscious. Returning to the guns I looked across the fifty yards to 378. Harvey was lying on the ground, he wasn't moving.

Salvoes of 4.2s and the smaller pip squeaks were now coming over and it became difficult for me to detect any one with our name on it.

Our luck came to an end when a small shell, probably a 4.2, landed by my corporal's gun, wounding two of his gunners. Mercifully their injuries were slight so I asked the corporal to take them back for first aid. There was nothing more he could do; he couldn't continue to fire because his gun had lost a wheel.

As I approached the other gun to reassure Sergeant Stevenson about the gunners' injuries, an HV pitched into the pile of shrapnel shells in front of me. Nothing happened ... a dud ... Then all hell was let loose as its lethal vibrations exploded our own shells. Down went Stevenson. Number Two was hurtled backwards. I started forward to help them as another dud landed at my feet and threw me to the ground ... I struggled up to find all four gunners felled by our own ammunition ... I stood alone – utterly devastated.

Suddenly I heard a massive salvo coming towards us. Demented I dived into my funk hole shouting "COVER!" although there was no one left to hear. There were ear-splitting crashes as shells fell everywhere. I felt sure one had got the mess. Earth poured into my funk hole and empty shell cases rolled on top of me until I could scarcely move. After a few minutes the din subsided. I eased myself out fearful that I was the only one alive. Dazed I got to my feet and looked around – the tarpaulin was still on the mess – there must be someone there – I staggered the few yards, opened the flap and looked in. Gardner was on a stretcher, Major Nicol of 376 was lying beside him. Smith and other subalterns crouched in the hole.

All were in hysterics, sobbing without restrain. Grimly determined not to give way I acted like a mad man. We were still on SOS. Rushing to the gun where my men lay dead, I yelled:

"SOS three thousand yards, three rounds a minute."

Stepping over the body of Sergeant Stevenson, I put a shell

in the breech. As I was about to elevate the gun I noticed that the clinometer was broken so I raised the barrel to make sure that the shell would be certain to clear our infantry. Then I fired. The noise and vibration were shattering. I hadn't fired a gun since I'd been a cadet at Larkhill.

The bang of the gun brought out the Sergeant Major and a gunner to see what was happening.

"We are still on SOS," I told them.

They then found two more gunners and managed to put another gun into action. The other batteries remained silent. The enemy had ceased fire. The balloon began to descend. I thought bitterly, "Coming down for lunch after a good shoot."

It was over – stupid to go on firing when all was quiet.

"Cease fire," I shouted.

I covered the bodies of Sergeant Stevenson and his gunners with their capes.

Now at the end of my tether with distress and fatigue, I must have collapsed, for the next thing I remember was Sutherland talking on the 'phone ordering me to go to the wagon line at Boves for a rest. I shall never forget that day. Others talk of "The Twelfth" and think of a grouse moor. For me "The Twelfth" is 12 April, 1918 – Hangard.

At Boves we were housed in bell tents. I had a really good sleep and was well fed. The banks of the Avre were green and lush. There were willow trees with newly opened leaves and Australians throwing grenades into the water to bring out a supply of fresh fish. I made several visits to Old Boy, who was still painfully thin. I patted him, spoke soothing words and fed him with a few handfuls of weeds. He nuzzled my hand, almost as if he was comforting me.

Wrapped in grief and despondency I was almost out of my mind. It is possible that here I was told about Gough's dismissal – that we had now become the Fourth Army under General Sir Henry Rawlinson – that the French General Foch had become overall commander of the French and British forces – and that the Hun had launched a successful attack further north. But if

I did learn of these events nothing registered. I was incapable of any thoughts. Certainly I didn't realize that the setback in the north meant that Rue Flourie was now in enemy hands. All I wanted was news of the Brigade and to rejoin what was left of it. I questioned everyone who came back from the front. Soon enough I learned of our heavy losses. Amongst the dead: Stevenson, who had taken the place of Watson at Cambrai, was one of the best gunners we ever had; Harvey of 378 whose bereaved family I was to meet several years later; my other gunners, and many more friends whose names I cannot recall.

Gardner, one of the kindest men I have ever met, was wounded. Although by training and temperament totally unsuited to warfare, he had been a good CO holding us together in most difficult circumstances. Wise enough to delegate gunnery decisions to Smith and myself he was no shirker and would have taken full responsibility for any mistakes. He would be missed by everyone in the Battery. I never heard what became of him. Over the years I have often looked at his drawings and hoped he was able to go again to church in his top hat. Our bitterness at the needless slaughter never left us. In his book Gibbs wrote:

Who was that dissatisfied "someone" who, having looked at a map from the safety of a back area, would not listen to the report of two Majors, one a regular who had visited the ground and spoke from their bitterly-earned experience? Do the ghosts of those officers and men, unnecessarily dead, disturb his rest o' nights, or is he proudly wearing another ribbon for distinguished service? Even from the map he ought to have known better. It was the only place where a fool would have put guns.

My comment written in 1920 in the margin of Gibbs' book reads "This was Hell". It is underlined.

Next day I rejoined the Brigade now in its previous position near Gentelles. There was little time for talk but I do remember being shown Haig's famous order of the day. The passage which I have remembered over the years commanded us to stand fast with our backs to the wall. The reaction was one of bewilderment. Wasn't that what we'd been doing since we'd left Essigny? I doubt whether we derived inspiration from the instruction but it did provide material for a few grim jokes.

With hindsight it appears that by issuing the order Haig may have had more than one objective. By spelling out what the British forces had already accomplished and noting that "the French Army is moving rapidly to our support" implying that they had done precious little to date, perhaps he was taking the opportunity to have a sly dig at Foch, who was now his superior officer.

The Brigade had been patched up and put into action within a couple of days. 377 Battery had gone. Our few survivors together with raw recruits newly arrived from England made up the number of the other three. Another colonel, also in France for the first time, took over from Sutherland. The Australian sergeant major had been moved to another battery, which was fair enough as we still had our own excellent sergeant major who'd been with us from the beginning.

My first assignment on return to the Brigade was to act as liaison officer. The attacks and counter-attacks had continued, making it difficult to obtain accurate information about SOS lines, so Sutherland decided that I should go forward to see what I could learn at the Australian HQ, now situated in Hangard Wood. I set off across the mutilated countryside. The debris of war, now only too familiar, no longer shocked. Near the wood there were apologies for trenches, merely shell holes joined together, and ahead grim reminders that the infantry had fought this ground yard by yard. Still wrapped in my own misery, I was almost indifferent to the grisly scene, but on reaching the skeleton trees and battered undergrowth I was shaken to the core. Never before or since have I seen such horror as was there in Hangard Wood. After three weeks of fierce fighting there were left, unburied, hundreds of dead.

British, French and German soldiers sprawled side by side, sometimes body on body, in varying stages of decay. I cannot find words to describe the holocaust. The stench was abominable. Fighting an overwhelming desire to turn and run I had to force myself on.

The HQ was established less than half way through Hangard Wood. The Australians were friendly but could give little useful information about their front. Patrols were going forward whenever the opportunity arose: there was no possibility of an SOS line. The Australians were in good spirits and remarkably optimistic despite their grim surroundings.

I did learn more about what had happened on 12 April. The Australians had heard that our artillery brigade had been wiped out but, they told me, we had given valuable support in the early morning helping to mow down the advancing Boche. The day had started badly particularly on the right where by noon the enemy had captured Hangard but by evening a brilliant counter-attack (I learned later that this was by the 10th Essex supported by the French) had regained the village.

It was some comfort to learn that 12 April had ended well enough and that we'd made a small contribution but I still felt bitter, firmly believing that we should have remained in our previous position near Gentelles and that we had been sacrificed because of the whim of some ignorant commander.

It wasn't until very recently that it occurred to me that had the weather on that crucial day continued unsettled, leaving us hidden under a blanket of mist, and if the Hun had not merely taken Hangard but had then gone on to advance along the road to Amiens, we would have been in an ideal position to mop him up on open sights – just as we'd done at Gonnelieu and Essigny. That brass hat may not have been an insensitive fool. He may well have known the risks, the possible cost in human life – he may well even have had a relative somewhere in the line with us. Poor man! I would not now grudge him a ribbon.

However, these were not my thoughts as I retraced my steps through the rotting flesh in Hangard Wood. We felt bitter and went on feeling bitter.

During the next days the Boche renewed his efforts, determined to take the key towns of Villers Bretonneux and Hangard. He began to pound the area with high explosive phosgene and mustard gas.

377 went into action again. Sergeant Gray was training new NCOs and gunners as they fired at the enemy. We had our back to the wall all right. On 24 April the battle was intensified as the Germans mounted a full scale attack on Villers Bretonneux which was being defended by the Australians. We fired non stop and were ourselves subjected to heavy shelling. Villers Bretonneux fell. Early next morning the Australians succeeded in driving out the Jerries. Our friends were jubilant.

Here is their version of events as told to us at the time. When they had first arrived at Villers Bretonneux they had found the cellars well stocked with wine. Unfortunately, they had done themselves too well and had been caught on the hop allowing Jerry to capture the town. This had been considered an appalling state of affairs, not to be tolerated. Jerry couldn't have all that wine. Just before midnight without waiting for orders, the Australians had attacked with anything they could lay their hands on – rifles, bayonets, revolvers and hand-grenades. With a total disregard for personal safety, they had dashed forward through the infilade fire with blood curdling yells, terrifying the Germans out of their wits. By the early hours of 25 April, most of the enemy had been driven out. The victors' only problem: sharing out the wine cellars amongst themselves.

The story lost nothing in the telling: we loved it. We didn't mind how often it was repeated, the more embellishments the better. I believe it did more for morale than dozens of orders of the day.

There is a more detached version of events in the history books. Jerry had prepared the attacks on Villers Bretonneux and Hangard with his customary thoroughness. What is particularly interesting is that for the first time he had employed tanks. In fact the tanks had rolled up almost to Cachy, within a mile of us. It was they who had shepherded the enemy into Villers Bretonneux. Fortunately, the Germany commander had been as unconvinced of the role of tanks as some of our commanders had been at Cambrai. Had he deployed these forerunners of the Panzer divisions with as much efficiency as he had trained his storm troopers for the 21 March, he might well have won the battle. As it was, the tank attack fizzled out. It is interesting to note that here had been the first encounter of tank with tank – won by the British, and also that our tanks had won a vital defensive action thanks to the vigilance of one of our aircraft observers in spotting advancing German infantry.

It should not be forgotten that as usual our ex-Fifth Army infantry had also played an important role in repelling the Hun. The French had played a lesser part but some days later they recaptured Hangard which had fallen, and after fierce fighting, their colonials, the Moroccans, supported by our guns, helped to complete the recapture of Hangard Wood, leaving more dead in that terrible graveyard.

However, there is little doubt that Australian brigades played a major role. Without their extraordinary courage Villers Bretonneux would have remained in enemy hands. No place in France is more closely associated with the Australians than Villers Bretonneux. After the war they gave money to rebuild the town and nearby erected a magnificent war memorial.

We Scots found much in common with the Australians, perhaps because in 377 relationships between officers and men were easy going; indeed regular army officers might have thought us something of an undisciplined rabble. However, we didn't carry informality to the same lengths as the Australians who regarded the acknowledgement of rank as an encumbrance; only their General Monash was graced with a title. He was a frequent visitor to our friends, as I believe he was to all his front-line troops. Their regard for him was little short of adulation – they called him "Mr" Monash. It was about this time that Smith and I began to address our own Major more informally, calling him Suthey (pronounced as in southerly).

We moved to the west of Villers Bretonneux where we were continuously on the alert, frequently in action. We staggered on with little or no sleep, munching iron rations when time allowed, wearing gas masks for long hours, diving into funk holes to avoid enemy shells. It seemed endless.

For me there is only one pleasant memory. Suthey and I were out on reconnaissance one day when a truck drew up beside us and an Australian officer asked the way to Amiens. We directed him to the main road. He drove on a few yards, stopped, leaned out and asked if either of us would like to accompany him: he'd only be gone a few hours. A few persuasive words from Suthey and I was on my way, delighted because previous visits to Amiens had been confined to the railway station.

In the town we drew up in front of the best hotel where the Australian suggested we should meet in an hour's time when he would have concluded his business. Meantime, he suggested I might like to have a look at the cathedral. Coming from Presbyterian Scotland, this was my first visit to a cathedral. I crossed a square towards the huge building with its twin towers. Sandbags protected the walls to a height of twenty feet or more and covered the main doorways; round one side I found an entrance. Shafts of sunlight filtered through the upper windows lighting the magnificent roof high above. I stood enthralled, the sheer size was bewildering, almost overpowering. I began to look around. The sumptuousness of the detail was astounding. I remember in particular the carving which adorned the choir and the exquisitely gilded statues.

The contrast to what I'd left behind an hour before was startling, incredible that a few miles away were horrors beyond description. It was so quiet. I experienced an extraordinary feeling of peace. Since witnessing the hell in Hangard Wood I'd found it difficult to believe in God. Now I could sit down and pray again. As I tried to explain to Suthey later it was like a renewal of faith.

Since that day I have visited many cathedrals – none has given the overwhelming sense of peace I experienced in the 13th-century cathedral of Amiens, truly "the peace of God which passeth all understanding".

Back in the hotel the Australian, having ordered a meal, was awaiting my return. The food was delicious; what a contrast to our meagre rations. The Aussie refused to let me share the bill and after all these years I cannot remember his name nor even his rank, though perhaps that's not surprising for an Australian. I only hope he knew how much I appreciated his thoughtful gesture in offering this trip to Amiens: for me it had proved far more significant than he could ever have realised.

Sometime in May we left our Australian friends and moved north to support the 18th Division, who were now holding the line on the west bank of the Ancre opposite Albert, which was then in German hands. We supported the infantry in raids on the enemy while our heavies poured shells into Albert, buildings disintegrating before our eyes. I remember seeing the famous tower of the church where the virgin – a gilded figure of the Madonna and child – had tilted into a precarious position during the early stages of the war. There had been a popular belief among the French that the day the figure fell the war would end, but the figure had fallen in March and the war was anything but over.

Our anxiety continued – the fear now being that the Hun was preparing another offensive for June. All we could do was to keep him busy so that he would be unable to withdraw his troops for training. We supported many raids on his positions while our heavies continued their task of reducing Albert to rubble. We were ill prepared for another attack with so many raw recruits and horses which were almost too feeble to move guns and ammunition from one place to another.

I was sorry for our new gunners – poor young fellows – to be thrown in at the deep end. For them no quiet front at Rue Flourie with time to practise on a disused ruin. Now it was register guns on the enemy infantry, on his gun positions, on his supply lines; with the rule changed from live and let live, to kill or you will be killed.

Once again we shared a mess with 379. I remember the spirited arguments which occupied the enforced breaks when we ran out of ammunition. Gibbs would lead one faction, Suthey the other. Since 12 April, Gibbs had come to believe, or so he said, that the time had come for us to lay down our arms and negotiate a truce with the German nation. Suthey argued that we had no alternative but to carry on, stick it out and win the war. We owed it to the men who had fallen he said. Needless to say I supported him. Like many others I had come to France to end the war by winning it; if that involved killing Germans or being killed myself, so be it. The debates continued intermittently for days. For the most part they were good humoured although Gibbs did take to referring to "the blood-thirsty Major and his Lieutenant". With their considerable knowledge of literature and philosophy, tinged with a nice sense of humour, the oratory of Gibbs and Suthey was a delight, and strangely kept our minds alive while physically we could scarcely keep going.

But there was no disguising the fact that the outlook was grim indeed. Most of us believed that we would win the war but after how long – another year, perhaps two – and at what cost? Now I could understand Robbie Burns' gloomy philosophical conclusions in his lines to a field mouse:

But Mousie, thou art no thy lane,
In proving foresight may be vain;
The best laid schemes o' mice an' men
    Gang aft agley,
An' lea'e us nought but grief an' pain,
    For promis'd joy!

Still thou art blest, compar'd wi' me;
The present only toucheth thee:
But och! I backward cast my e'e,
On prospect drear!
An' forward, tho' I canna see,
I guess an' fear!

8

Out of the Line

Our ordeal continued, and we became so depleted we were
pulled out of the line. We moved back from the battle zone to
an area where farmers were working their fields, hoeing crops,
tending cattle, trying to ignore the war and above all wanting
nothing to do with marauding soldiers of any nationality. We
were camped on a small farm and as a matter of courtesy
Suthey paid the farmer a visit. Upon returning, Suthey told us
that the farmer had been gruff and off hand but his daughter
friendly and anxious to please.

We would have ignored the neighbouring farmers if it hadn't
been for our half starved horses. Still very short of fodder we
pleaded with the farmers for hay but few of them would help us
and those who did demanded an extortionate price which we
had to pay out of our own pockets.

Within a week a brass hat rolled up in a motor car to inspect
the horses. Far from being sympathetic as expected, after seeing
the horses he scolded:

"Appalling – pitiful – quite the worst condition of horses I've
ever seen; a disgraceful case of neglect."

Totally ignoring our lack of rations during the exhausting
retreat, he issued an exceedingly rude reprimand somehow
suggesting that the poor animals were suffering because of our
lack of care. Suthey, holding himself carefully in hand, calmly
asked for advice on how we could obtain more forage. The

brass hat blustered for a moment, then exclaimed:

"Nettles, nettles – you must cut nettles. Feed them on nettles." He then quickly departed in his motor car.

I will not elaborate on what was said after this inspection. As for the nettles, there were a few along the lanes but not enough to feed ten horses let alone a hundred. Still, orders were orders.

Where could we find a scythe to cut the nettles? "Leave it to me," said Suthey, and went off again to see the farmer. It wasn't long before he was back with the information that the farmer had a scythe but had refused to hand it over. However, Suthey had managed to see the daughter on her own and had invited her to the mess for a drink. That evening we assembled to greet our guest. She turned out to be a good looking woman but it was Suthey with his fluent French who made all the running. Presently he explained the difficulty regarding the scythe and asked for her help, whereupon she offered to bring her father to the mess because she was sure he would enjoy our whisky and we could try again to borrow "la faux".

Suthey made careful preparation for the farmer's visit. It was most important, he felt, that in order to get the farmer well oiled we should ensure that he drank his whisky like wine – neat. In case he became suspicious I was instructed to do the same. The only previous time I'd taken more than a double nip neat was on that troublesome journey to Cambrai with the caravan. As that hadn't done any real harm, I promised to cooperate.

The farmer and his daughter arrived next evening. Suthey proceeded to pour nearly half a pint of whisky into the farmer's glass and a similar quantity into mine. Unobtrusively he produced a second bottle from which he filled his own and the daughter's glass with watered down whisky. Then he toasted our French guests and added, "Damnation to the Boche."

The party went with a swing and in due course the farmer was persuaded to lend us "la faux". Dutifully I kept pace with the farmer drinking my whisky like wine. However, the time came when I felt that a retreat would be prudent. I managed to

140

reach my tent and crawl into my valise before blacking out.

Next morning I was awakened by a triumphant Suthey with the news that the Battery had acquired a scythe. I must admit I wasn't very enthusiastic, feeling rather the worse for wear. It wasn't long before the farmer's daughter arrived waving her arms and shouting.

"Quel malheur, quel malheur. Mon père est très malade."

I wasn't surprised.

Using the scythe, our pocket knives and even cooking utensils we spent all day cutting nettles. Finally we had a heap of about forty pounds for the day's work. All that effort had produced less than half a pound for each horse. It was perhaps fortunate that the next day we received news that the Brigade was to move back forty miles to a camp near Abbeville. A real rest at last – this was welcome news indeed.

We took four days to reach our destination, making leisurely progress for the sake of the horses, who this time had an easy journey with no ammunition in the wagons. Each night we stayed in billets or bivouacs. I have cause to remember the last night of that journey because Old Boy disappeared.

Sergeant Gray was furious. He was certain that Old Boy had been stolen by Australians who were in the vicinity. He asked if he could go to their camp to make enquiries. I too was upset, but I wasn't going to let Sergeant Gray go anywhere near the Australians whose peacetime livelihood depended on their wits and physical prowess. He wouldn't stand a chance.

The unfortunate driver who had been on picket duty was paraded for a dressing down. Poor fellow; Old Boy had been tethered near the road at the end of a horse line, it must have been quite easy for some wily Aussie to slip him loose.

Sergeant Gray found me a handsome black charger but I sorely missed Old Boy who during so many ordeals had been my friend and companion.

The rest camp was in a pleasant position near a lagoon, a backwater of the Somme. The horse lines were established in a large field protected by woods on three sides. The horses of 377

Battery formed a double line up the left-hand side. Guns, limbers and wagons were lined up in another field nearby. For the first time the officers of all four batteries shared a mess presided over by the Colonel.

Within a day of our arrival a notice appeared on the board in the mess to the effect that a special week's leave was available for war weary officers, two per battery. No one was keen to take it, assuming that by doing so any normal leave would be delayed. But Smith and I thought differently.

"We may not live to get another," we said. So I went home to Barras and spent three days and nights with my wife and family. Real food, real beds with clean sheets and blankets: it was another world. No one could understand what it had been like out there and I couldn't begin to describe it. There were no TV crews in Hangard Wood to take angled shots of skeletons and blasted trees, no close-ups of headless corpses, no lenses to zoom in on rats swarming over human flesh – no recordings of the shattering blast of guns nor of the shouts, the screams, the moans of the dying. I couldn't describe it to them – in the end I said very little.

Back in Abbeville, the Brigade had been making the most of the break. There had been attempts at spit and polish but also there had been time for swimming, playing football and visiting Abbeville for shopping and concerts. Now we had an opportunity to explore the countryside and to sit and indulge in idle conversation.

It was during one of these periods that Suthey happened to mention that an MC had come up with the rations and the Colonel, being new to the Brigade had asked for guidance about its allocation. Suthey was inclined to think it should go to the Adjutant whose tireless efforts had done so much to ensure our safe withdrawal after 21 March. What did Smith and I think? Certainly the Adjutant had done splendid work but I was in no doubt about the allocation of the MC: it should go to George Harvey of 378, who on 12 April had, without regard for his own safety, come out to rally his men when all his guns were silent. Suthey then agreed saying that he had been told that on 21 March Harvey's contribution as Forward Observation Officer of 378 had been invaluable.

Some years later, when working in Cheshire, I was to worship at St Mary's Parish Church in Nantwich. My eyes often strayed to a plaque on the sandstone wall which read:

To the glory of God and in memory of Lt. G.W. Harvey, MC.

I would read it and visualize him – I still can – standing on a heap of upturned earth, bravely ignoring enemy shells. For me, his action symbolized the courage of all my fellow gunners who, on 12 April, 1918, stood fast and paid with their lives.

Before our rest period came to an end, we were informed that Sir Douglas Haig was to pay us a visit of inspection. Very few were honoured in this way. Apparently, it was because our Brigade was one of the few who had brought back its guns after 21 March.

You can imagine the spit and polish which preceded the visit. As I was Brigade orderly officer of the day I was up at dawn. Horses, now looking better after being allowed to graze freely on land in the vicinity, were groomed until their coats shone. Guns, limbers and wagons were immaculate.

The Field Marshal was due to arrive at 2 p.m. The Colonel and all the officers of the Brigade lunched early. Afterwards, whilst waiting for the great event a stupid young subaltern messing about with his revolver managed to put a bullet through his foot. The Colonel and battery commanders were panic stricken. There was a terrible commotion: this sort of thing was regarded with suspicion and was therefore much more difficult to explain away than if a dozen men had been killed in action. I decided to get out of the way.

The mess was set back from the road on the opposite side to where the horses and wagons awaited inspection. As I crossed the road to the horse lines a party of men on horseback appeared from the left. The uniforms were unmistakable – top brass. The great man had arrived twenty minutes early.

The party came to a halt a few yards away. I sprang to attention and saluted. Field Marshal Haig showed no surprise at being received by a mere subaltern. He rode forward on his magnificent charger and said:

"Will you show me your horses?"

I led him to the 377 lines on the left. Walking alongside his horse I escorted him to the top of the field. He said something like:

"You must have had a rough time during the retreat."

I found myself telling him that both men and horses had survived ten days with little or no food: at the end we were all worn out but, I added, the men had recovered more quickly than the horses which for weeks had been nothing but skin and bone. We reached the end of the line and turned to come down the next row. Haig looked carefully at all the horses.

"They seem to be recovering," he said.

I am certain his concern for their welfare was genuine. In all, he spent at least half an hour on the double row of horses taking his time to study each one in turn. He said nothing to the men. When we reached the road the Colonel and battery commanders were waiting. Very embarrassed, they stood to attention and saluted while I did my best to melt into the background. Haig spent a few moments talking to the Colonel and then to everyone's disappointment rode on. But the Commander-in-Chief's visit wasn't the last excitement of the day. Later that afternoon I came across Sergeant Gray shepherding towards the wood two of our drivers, each leading a magnificent Clydesdale horse. The Clydesdales had wandered unaccompanied into our horse lines, and Sergeant Gray was having them removed out of sight some two hundred yards away amongst the trees. After some hesitation, I decided to turn a blind eye.

Before it was dark I made a final round of the lines where I found Sergeant Gray listening sympathetically to some Australians – poor fellows, they had lost two Clydesdale horses. We were very short of heavy horses and we kept those

144

Clydesdales until the end of the war but at any time I would have willingly exchanged them for Old Boy.

After a few more days we set off on our forty-mile trek back to the line. We were in remarkably good shape, almost completely recovered from the two-month long action which had followed 21 March. Now it was the middle of June. It was just as well we were fit. The war was anything but over.

9

Holding On

We rejoined the line again near Albert but this time opposite the river Ancre further south than our previous position. It was a countryside of sharply rising small hills deeply cut by valleys with little streams tumbling down to the main river across which the opposing armies kept an uneasy vigil.

During our absence the sector had seen a series of minor attacks by the Germans and counter-attacks by the Allies, but there had been no further major push by the Germans. Instead the Germans had turned their attention much further south where they had gained a sizeable triangle of territory between Montdidier, Rheims and Château Thierry, the last of these being only fifty-six miles from Paris. This advance had been checked by French and British divisions which had been moved south for a rest in a 'quiet sector', and an American division which had been in the area on a training exercise.

The question in everyone's mind was where would the Germans strike next? From the Channel ports to the Swiss border the Allies were on the alert. A game of bluff and counter-bluff began to develop with the Germans apparently preparing to attack one sector then another, while the Allies simulated defensive strength where there was weakness and weakness where there was strength. Soon a second and more cheering question was to be heard: when would the Allies, now including the Americans, be ready to take the initiative? We guessed this move was some time distant, but that it would come, we were confident. Meantime we only hoped we'd survive to see it.

Our first assignment was to relieve a battery which had suffered heavy casualties during a Boche assault on a small salient. We arrived in time for the counter-attack which was to include a bombardment. An inspection of the position, placed typically behind a crest, confirmed that Fritz had it bracketed, fresh shell holes everywhere – not an encouraging prospect. – It could be 12 April all over again, to be offering ourselves as target for German guns which could be certain to retaliate when we opened up. Suthey was on leave so it was for Smith and I to see what could be done to avert such a disaster. There was one possibility. If at nightfall we placed the guns in front of the crest directly in line with the previous position we'd have less cover but Fritz might remain ignorant of what we had done and assume gun flashes were coming from behind the crest. It was a chance worth taking. As soon as it was dark we moved up the guns to the theoretically more vulnerable position in front of the crest.

At Zero we commenced gun fire at four rounds a minute. Soon enough we heard pip squeaks and 4.2s on their way. Every one of them whizzed overhead and landed behind the crest. We didn't lose a man but the other batteries, all of which had taken up positions previously occupied, suffered casualties. Before daylight all moved back well behind the line.

Before we came into action again we were struck down by another enemy, a most virulent form of influenza virus. Most of the gunners ran high temperatures and were very ill indeed. We crowded them into bell tents while the few of us who were lucky enough to escape the infection slept outside on the ground, on hand to carry drinks of water and do what we could to help. We had a very anxious few days before the crisis passed and the invalids began to recover. There was a small consolation in that we heard that the Boche was suffering too. Eventually we were back on our feet and reasonably fit.

Others were not so lucky. The virus had struck world wide and soon letters began to arrive from home with distressing news of the deaths of relatives and friends. In fact, that epidemic of 1918 was one of the severest holocausts of disease ever. In Britain there were 144,000 deaths. World wide there were over 20 million.

It wasn't long before we were back at the front taking part in an intensive bombardment of enemy targets. I don't know how long it lasted but we became very tired. Short of officers and men we went days without sleep. Eventually, I was so worn out I had to find someone to take over. I remember it was raining at the time and Duncan, who had been up with the guns, led me back to a bivvie which he'd found in a bank. There under the cover of a corrugated iron sheet I could have a proper sleep. Gratefully I climbed in, flopped down on a ground sheet and sank into oblivion.

Duncan tugged at my arm. Half conscious I heard him tell me I was wanted at the guns. Blinking at my watch I saw that I'd had ten minutes rest. I will not repeat what was said as I struggled out of the bivvie.

At the guns there was some query about targets. A few 4.2s fell around the position as I sorted out the problem but no one was hurt. At last the guns were aligned to everyone's satisfaction and I could return to the make-shift bedroom. But when I reached it I found that the bankside had been rent asunder, for during my enforced absence the bivvie had taken a direct hit. I don't know who was the more shaken, Duncan or me.

This personal episode is all I remember of the diversionary battery work in which I believe we were engaged during the battle for Hamel which had fallen to the Germans two months previously. Being on high ground overlooking the outskirts of Villers Bretonneux, this village had been a hazard to the Australians ever since. Meticulous preparations for the recovery of Hamel had involved all the fighting services, including tanks and the whole operation had been co-ordinated by Rawlinson and Monash. It is interesting to note that here for the first time American infantry had lined up alongside the British. Bearing this in mind Rawlinson's choice of 4 July, American Independence Day, for the commencement of battle had been an imaginative gesture. The operation was a success and a superb example of co-operation between the fighting services and with hindsight it can be seen as a prototype for the Allied attacks which were to follow. But Jerry was far from beaten. We fired almost non stop, searching and sweeping the river valley for any position where he might be preparing an offensive. On at least one occasion he nearly broke through.

Rumours spread that Jerry was preparing a tank attack. By now it was recognized that the most effective anti-tank weapon was an eighteen-pounder on open sights and it had become the practice for one or two guns from a division to be moved near the front where they could be hidden yet have a wide open field of fire. It was a do or die assignment. An order came through to our battery – we were to provide and man one of these guns. Having had adequate experience of firing on open sights, I was chosen for this unenviable job.

During daylight I went forward to reconnoitre a suitable site. Towards the foot of a hillside near the Ancre, I found an open field bordered by a hedge. At one side there was a low bank. With luck, we could remain behind this, hidden from German field glasses which would be scanning the area on the look out for defensive positions.

At dark we took up a gun and ammunition, shrapnel for raiding Jerry infantry, HE for tanks. We took great pains with our camouflage, thickening up the hedge with branches of a similar species cut from one further back. Several times I crawled into the field to check that what we had done appeared absolutely natural. We settled down to await the dawn, praying for the absence of early morning fog when our fire would be useless and annihilation almost certain. Morning came. Anxiously we peered into mist but nothing happened.

Day followed day; we continued to man our gun. The

weather was splendid. During daylight we slept in turns lying in the open, shaded from the sun by the camouflage net, happy to escape the roar of guns and the smell of cordite. When night fell we replaced the wilting branches in our hedge and braced ourselves for what the dawn might bring. At the end of a week others took our place. So far as I knew they had no trouble either. Jerry must have changed his mind.

During the next fortnight we remained near the Ancre. Several times we were moved forward to take part in a particular action and then almost immediately were pulled back again to resume our routine of searching and sweeping.

I remember that on one occasion we went forward to help our infantry who were having trouble from German machine-guns in a hut on the other side of the river. The only place from which this hut was visible was a slight knoll in the middle of a field of ripening barley which lay beyond our infantry, sloping down to the river in full view of the Hun. To direct fire on the machine-gunners it would be necessary to establish an OP on the knoll. Two signallers and I prepared to go forward. We pulled up barley by the roots and tied it round our persons. Helped by the signallers, I spent some time arranging the stalks round my tin hat until barley appeared to be growing from my head – I paid special attention to my hands and wrists, so that when we reached the OP. I would not only be able to lift my head but also raise my field glasses undetected.

When we were ready we went forward with a drum of wire for keeping touch with the Battery. Inch by inch we snaked through the barley. Eventually, we reached the knoll. Carefully I put up my head and raised my glasses. There was a splendid view of the German hut up the hillside across the river. Orders were relayed by the signallers: range, HE, one gun, one round. We wanted the operation to appear as casual bursts of sporadic fire not an organized attack which would bring retaliation. Our first shot landed beyond the target. We made our correction and waited for a good ten minutes.

"Fire," a pause – the shell sped over the valley.

I saw the hut go up in the air in a cloud of dust before the noise came echoing back. We lay motionless in the barley for half an hour before we snaked our way back to safety.

On return from this expedition, I went straight to the mess to clean up. There I found Suthey with an officer newly arrived from cadet school. After introductions Suthey, knowing that I would be going to congratulate the gunners, suggested that I take the young man along to have a look round. As we went out towards the gun positions Jerry decided to retaliate. As the shell came over I dropped flat to the ground. The shell landed some thirty yards behind us. I got to my feet and noting that the new officer had remained standing told him that whenever he heard a shell coming he should get down quickly – it was our usual practice. He was a very tall young man, he looked down at me in disbelief as clearly he thought that things were coming to a pretty pass with the war being fought by these windy old fellows. Patiently I made another attempt, explaining the dangers of splinters and flying debris, adding that this was one of the survival drills not taught at cadet school. The words were scarcely out of my mouth when another shell came towards us – down I flopped. After the dust cleared I got up to find the young man still on his feet but clutching his head moaning in agony. A splinter had gone in through one cheek and out at the other. It was a blighty one and we never saw him again.

We were very short of officers and matters were not helped by the brass hats who, I believe, out of kindness of heart were doing their best to see that those who had been through the thick of it were receiving their allocation of leave. Back again from the front we found on offer a week-end leave in Paris. I'd never visited the French capital so decided to apply. This request was no sooner granted than my normal leave came through. Apparently, the war weary officers' leave, enjoyed from Abbeville, had been an extra. I had two days sightseeing in Paris, then went home to Barras.

10

On the Offensive

I returned from leave on 4 August to find Amiens unusually busy with senior commanders round every corner. No one appeared to know exactly what was going on and it took some time to discover that 169 Brigade was hidden in a wood about three miles west of Ribemont, a village on the Ancre.

The gunners were bursting with news of a trip north to St Omer. They had travelled at night by train with all guns and equipment. For several days on this northern front, in full daylight, the whole outfit had moved from one site to another. Then under cover of darkness they had been entrained back to Amiens. Now there were strict orders – keep out of sight – no movement during daylight – no discussion, but despite these attempts at secrecy, rumours were rife that big guns were arriving by train and being hidden in the neighbourhood. It was obvious that we were preparing to attack. On the evening of 6 August we learned that we were about to move.

We may have known that 376 and 379 had already moved up to the Ancre but what we didn't know was that earlier that day they had been in action when Jerry had mounted a surprise attack along the river valley from Ville to Ribemont. Our infantry had been forced to retreat, a serious setback, but finally the attack had been checked. Troops, which should have been in reserve, were now moving up to the front to retake the lost ground as we were about to leave our hiding place.

We emerged from the wood in darkness. Obeying instructions we had taken every precaution to deaden the sound of our vehicles, wrapping sacks round the wheels and binding any part of the harness which might jingle. Without a single light we followed a hilly track round to our new position just back from the river in the neighbourhood of Ribemont. On arrival there was much to do. Guns were dug in with as little disturbance of the soil as possible – tracks marks were obliterated – there were constant checks on camouflage. Then of course there was ammunition to stack, wagon load after wagon load came up, and we went on working through the next day doing our best to keep out of sight. At nightfall we subalterns each received a map and our orders. As at Cambrai no registration. Aiming posts to be set up by map and compass, zero four o'clock next morning, four rounds per minute on an enemy trench for ten minutes, then a creeping barrage of two rounds a minute as ordered.

But unlike Cambrai there were so many last minute preparations that we went on working through the night. This time there was no uneasy silence as the hours ticked away towards zero for already there was a scrap in progress on our right flank and beyond it the unmistakable rumble of a bigger battle. As dawn approached mist shrouded the valley. We saw no tanks, nor any of our infantry and we heard no planes.

Zero – a roar much more deafening than Cambrai – again we were taken by surprise, we had no idea so many guns had come up. Unlike the opening of Cambrai there was no elation only a grim satisfaction that we were having another go, we knew only too well what might happen. It was more like 21 March with the positions reversed.

Our barrage moved forward hundreds of yards as the infantry advanced according to plan. About 10 a.m. there was a hold up. Our barrage had moved too far ahead of the infantry who had run into trouble – we were ordered to reduce range by four hundred yards – concentrate on a map square and then fire again, zero – 12.15 p.m. – presumably when the infantry were ready to renew their attack. Our orders were twenty rounds of gun-fire – an unusually intense assault – then add one hundred. This took place. For the remainder of the day we put down harassing fire on further enemy concentrations.

On 9 August we fired in support of our infantry who, unknown to us, were making a successful attack on Morlancourt. On 10 August we began to feel apprehensive as rumours spread of a sizeable advance made over on our right by the Australians and Canadians. Why hadn't we advanced? What had gone wrong? We felt most uneasy.

However, later that day our anxiety eased when we received orders to be ready to move. During the night we set off. Led by the wagons of Brigade HQ we crossed the river and turned left up the valley. It was pitch dark. Several times we halted and it was difficult to judge distance although within a mile we turned right along a road with rising ground on the left and a ten foot high bank on our right. Presently on our left we came to a perpendicular rock face of some thirty feet, where we halted. Then upwards for a quarter of a mile to an open space to be informed that this was our new gun site. The guns were to be aligned on the north-east side of the hill which had been on our left as we came up from the valley. Behind us and off to the right of the road there was a ravine or gully. It was decided that I should go and reconnoitre this gully to find a place for a mess while Suthey and Smith would see to the guns. Meantime Brigade HQ left us and went a few yards further on beyond the hill on our left.

On investigation the gully proved to be wide, probably fifty yards at the entrance, with a stream flowing down the middle. On the right there was a very steep bank and various obstructions, so I kept to the left on an easier slope. Within twenty yards I was stopped in my tracks by a most appalling stench. I recognized it instantly – the grim stench of Hangard Wood. I braced myself for the horror – mutilated bodies rotting where they had fallen. Further on I crossed to the other side where I'd noticed dugouts at the foot of the steep bank and here too were many dead, all Germans.

I climbed to a parapet at the top of the bank noting many small shell holes; probably the result of our gunfire on 8 August when the enemy had held up our infantry. Beyond the parapet there was a large open field or plateau of about ten acres over which our men must have had to advance. No wonder they'd had trouble.

It was difficult to find a site for the mess away from the offensive smell. After carefully noting the direction of the wind I chose a small bay in the left-hand bank, and for the bivvies a place nearer to the guns at the entrance to the gully. It took all day to complete our digging of these places. In fact our new position was north-east of Morlancourt on the west side of the higher ground which lies between the Somme and the Ancre. I doubt whether we were aware then that there was no infantry between us and the enemy. We and 169 Brigade HQ were in the front line.

In the evening as we were munching our rations the

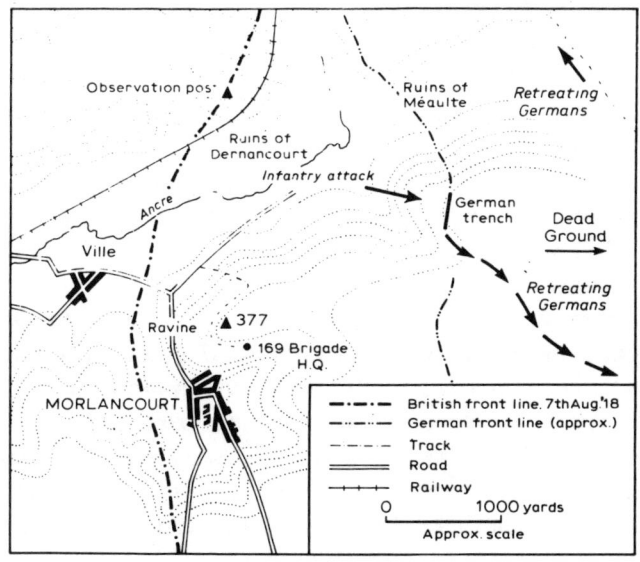

On the offensive, August 1918

155

Adjutant arrived on foot from Brigade HQ which, we now learned, was not far distant. We discovered that the other batteries which had moved a day or two previously were over on our right.

The Adjutant handed some papers to Suthey saying:

"Here's something from Corps." Then he explained further.

"The Brigade has to carry out a creeping barrage in front of infantry and tanks tomorrow at three p.m. By eleven a.m. you must have an officer and signallers at an OP across the river and they must be in communication with your battery." Suthey looked at me and said:

"Carlos, this will be a job for you."

We all looked for the map square and found the position for the OP on a hill at the other side of the Ancre valley about a mile and a half distant. The Adjutant continued his instructions.

"The officer at the OP must give a full report but under no circumstances can he direct fire from any gun. The barrage will be directed by Corps."

"That's unusual," commented Suthey.

The Adjutant took back the papers he had handed to Suthey and found the relevant passage. He read it out slowly and distinctly:

"The officer at the OP must give a full report but under no circumstances can he direct fire from any gun. The barrage will be directed by Corps."

Early next morning two signallers and I set off carrying two large drums of wire which we laid along the ditch on the left-hand side of the track up which we'd come at night. We reached the main road in the Ancre valley and threaded our wire through a culvert to keep it safe from tanks or other vehicles. The Ancre was exceptionally low after the recent hot weather so we were able to keep our feet dry by stepping from one stone to another. We crossed the river and a derelict railway and were then faced by steeply rising ground covered by patches of gorse, so we made our way round to the left into

156

a small valley where we could easily climb the hillside. At the top we turned right into a grassy hollow which had been an old trench. We followed this to our map square and then made contact with the battery. I reported that I had a clear view of the spur to be attacked which was a mile distant on the other side of the valley, but I couldn't see the Battery for the corner of the hill in front of it.

Within a few minutes, from the other side of the hill behind the OP, a party of senior American officers appeared. Apparently they had come from Corps to observe the creeping barrage. Their own field-guns had not yet arrived, but American infantry was now in the line. After saluting they gave us a friendly greeting but didn't tell us why they had come. They began to wander about all over the place whereupon, fearful that they would be seen by Jerry, I suggested that they might care to join us in the trench, an invitation which they politely declined. With my glasses I scanned the enemy territory across the valley, anxiously searching for enemy positions which might pick off these innocent observers. There was none to be seen. What I did see was a trench at the top of the spur with Jerry helmets moving about in it. Mercifully, we were just out of rifle and machine-gun range or they would soon have had our American friends scurrying for cover. There was no fire on us at all and I soon realized that the Germans must have withdrawn their field-guns for without any shadow of doubt there would be one of their observers on that hill behind the spur who would have reported our presence to a Field Artillery Battery had there been one in the vicinity.

The Americans asked a lot of questions. In particular they wanted to know the exact position of our guns; as these were hidden by the corner of the hill I couldn't show them the exact place, nor where they were registered. The Americans scanned the German trench with interest and suggested that I should shoot it up. I had to explain that we were under Corps command and that I was expressly forbidden to direct fire from any gun. Nevertheless, watched by the Americans, I took out my protractor and filled in the time making a careful calculation of the range and switch which would align our guns on the trench at the top of the spur, as it seemed obvious that we would have to clear it of Jerries.

Our tanks and infantry were due to assemble on a road at the bottom of the slope which led up to this position. Again and again I scanned the area which was to receive our creeping barrage – that up the slope between the road and the enemy trench. The spur rose steeply to within four hundred yards of the trench, then it became a gentle slope on which our infantry would be in full view of the Jerries.

The Americans also scanned the area with their glasses. Like me they detected no movement except for activity in the German trench. It looked as if the Jerries were expecting an attack. Privately I thought they had been put on the alert by their observer on the hill above the trench who had not only spotted us, but had also seen movement from our tanks and infantry assembling below.

The time passed slowly. We sat in the sun, the friendly Americans plying us with cigarettes and food from their luncheon hamper. I was fascinated by their strange way of speech, which was totally unfamiliar to me – not having been raised in the world of film and radio.

2.55 p.m.: the infantry and the tanks would be lined up out of sight under the brow of the slope on the road. Exactly at 3 p.m. on the left of the hill the infantry appeared impressively spread out in a line about 150 yards long, each man five yards from the next. All at once I heard the eighteen-pounder shells on the way and saw them burst 50 yards ahead. I reckoned the guns were firing four rounds a minute. After three minutes they lifted 100 yards. The range seemed quite accurate as our men moved steadily up the slope. Soon they would be in sight of the trench. The tanks appeared to have stuck on the steep hillside. We could see the German helmets now absolutely still.

All at once, fire spurted from Jerry machine-guns. Some of our men fell, others went down on one knee, rifle at the ready, others crept along the ground. They didn't stand a chance against the Jerries in the trench above. I got on the 'phone to Suthey.

"The creeping barrage is useless; the enemy is concentrated in the trench 400 hundred yards ahead. Can I use the left section to knock them out? I can quote range and switch."

"I'll ask Corps," Suthey replied.

I thought the reply would never come. The attack couldn't possibly succeed as the tanks were stuck. They should have been up there sweeping into the trench. I was furious at this delay. The Americans were frantic.

"Fire, Gunner, fire," they shouted.

At last Suthey's answer.

"No – they won't give permission."

"Try again – please try again," I pleaded. "Our men are being slaughtered. The attack will fail completely if we don't shoot."

The Americans, now seething with anger, turned on me. I tried to explain that it was a Corps shoot under Corps command and that Corps had refused permission.

"Protest," they said, "make a protest." Someone muttered, "Tell them to go to Hell."

"I have protested," I said. "My Major would have given permission at once. Corps says 'no'. It's tragic."

It was too late. We watched our men retreating, leaving their dead, bringing down their wounded.

The language of the Americans was unprintable. What the Hell did we think we were doing? There had been no enemy where we'd put down the barrage. Why hadn't we done something about it? Once again, I explained that I had clear instructions. My orders were to observe the creeping barrage and make a report. Under no circumstances was I to direct the fire of a gun. All I could do now was send in a stinker of a report and damn the consequences.

"You'll be all right," muttered the senior American before he and his party departed over the hill.

For a time I just stood still. Feeling unreasonably guilty about what had happened, I resolved that I would be court martialled rather than hush things up.

"We'll go back now," I said to the signallers.

As we made our way down the hill winding the wire, I kept wondering what I could put on the report. How could I describe this senseless episode?

Suthey came out to meet us, distressed that he had been unable to get permission to fire on the trench. I described what had happened and told him what I had in mind to put in my report to Corps.

"Go ahead," he said.

I cannot recall exactly what I wrote. I complained that there must have been no reconnaissance of the position otherwise it would have been obvious that a creeping barrage would be ineffective with no enemy on the slope. The barrage did not get to within a hundred yards of the trench where the enemy was assembled and did nothing to prevent the casualties suffered by the infantry. Tanks could have dealt with the men in the trench but had been unable to negotiate the steep gradient. The situation could have been retrieved had I been given permission to fire on the trench with our guns. The exercise had been a hopeless failure resulting in needless loss of life.

That night I couldn't sleep. I find no words to describe my anger and distress as I thought of our men lying dead on the slopes north of Morlancourt. Next morning I braced myself for the reprimand from Corps and it wasn't long before a messenger arrived. I watched Suthey read the order; he gasped with astonishment.

"Carlos, have a look at this. You seem to have shaken them at Corps."

Carefully I read the order. I and my two signallers were to return to the OP, observe the attack which would resume at 2 p.m., and in place of a creeping barrage I could direct the fire of all the guns of the Brigade and if necessary call on Corps for help. When I looked up, Suthey was smiling.

"I don't think I'll need Corps. I can knock that damned trench to pieces with our own battery, but I'll know for certain when I register our guns on it," I told him.

We set off laying our line as before, cheered by this unexpected development. When we reached the OP we found the American officers waiting for us and they were brimming over with ill-concealed excitement. I suspected that they knew all about our orders but their first question was "What are you going to do?"

"I'm going to register my guns on that trench." Scanning it with my glasses I added. "I can see the Jerries are still there but they won't have it all their own way this afternoon."

A signaller reported, "We're through to Battery, Sir."

"Give the order 'left section prepare for action'," I replied.

I had of course worked out the range and switch the previous day but no harm in checking. American heads crowded over the large scale map as I spread it on the ground and proceeded to calculate the range – just over two thousand yards. It was easy to measure the switch but we were almost at right angles to the line of fire and it would be difficult to correct this if off target.

Once again I wrote down the range and switch in my log book. The Americans noticed that the entry was the same as that written yesterday.

"Yes," I said, "You'll be able to see what would have happened if I'd been allowed to fire." Now to register the guns:

"Left gun ten degrees three minutes left, range two thousand yards, one round HE."

Within a minute we heard the shell on its way; it landed about twenty yards short of the near end of the trench where a machine-gunner had been in action the previous day. There was a simultaneous shout from the Americans.

"Well done!"

"Add forty and repeat."

The next shell landed just over the trench.

"Register all guns ten degrees thirty minutes left, range two thousand and twenty."

161

The Americans wanted to know why I didn't fire on this range and switch and hit the trench there and then. I told them that there was no need for a further shot. I was confident that when the first volley was ordered it would land on the trench. I went on to explain that our guns were about twelve yards apart so that the first volley would cover the near half of the trench, which had been the more active yesterday. A switch of two minutes right would land on the far half.

The Americans were raring to go. I explained that it was perfectly possible to clear the trench now but if we did there couldn't be an attack at 2 p.m. I had to agree that if we didn't get the trench with the first volley we might suffer casualties but I must obey orders. I told them, "I'll give the order when I see the first flash of fire."

I rang up the battery again and told them to have at least twenty HE shells by each gun as I might require five shell volleys.

The sun shone on the hills in front and visibility was perfect. Looking around with my glasses I noticed there was some movement of men from the trench to a path which went to the dead ground (the ground we couldn't see), round the back of the hill. Beyond the dead ground all was closely wired except for one narrow road. I looked at my map, found the road and wondered whether it was within range of our guns. Yes, it was at extreme range six thousand yards. There seemed to be a steady stream of men going up and down, suggesting a concentration of enemy behind the hill. I drew the attention of the Americans to what I'd seen.

"The men in the trench will take that road when they retreat. I'm going to register the guns on it."

Again all heads over the map as I explained what I was going to do. The range was just over six thousand yards. I registered the first hundred-yard stretch of road which was just to the left of the hill. I used a 103 shell, which was one which when fired at long range, fell on its nose and burst when it touched the ground. Again I had the greatest luck with my ranging shots. I

162

registered this length of road as Target No. II and ordered the Battery to be prepared to give a burst of five rounds of gunfire, HE, 103 and to have at least another ten shells at hand.

The Americans were impressed by our display of accurate shooting (privately, so was I). They wanted to know how long it had taken to learn to register a target like this. I told them that I had been fortunate in spending a long time on a quiet front near Armentières where, when on OP duty, I'd often had permission to fire on dummy targets in the background.

"Why haven't you been in action?" someone asked.

"Oh," I said, "I've seen plenty of action but I've mostly registered targets by map and compass. I've rarely seen them, except on open sights."

Friendly relations with the Americans were completely restored after the débâcle of yesterday. Once again we ate our picnic lunch in the sunshine. Long before 2 p.m. we were keyed up and waiting. At 1.55 I gave the order:

"Battery stand by for five rounds gunfire on target number one."

The message came back: "Ready."

Zero! The infantry appeared magnificently in line. Still out of sight of the enemy trench, they started to move up the hill. But the Jerries must have been warned. All along the trench, the coal scuttle helmets appeared. I spotted a machine-gunner at the near end as he got his gun into position. Keeping my eyes on him I sent another message to our guns.

"Ready any minute now."

The machine-gunner was now absolutely still. Did he guess that over a mile away six guns were pointing in his direction? Did he banish thoughts of wife and children as he concentrated on the target appearing up the spur? A red spurt of flame flashed from his gun.

"Fire!" I shouted.

"Fire!" the signallers repeated the order.

Within seconds we could hear our shells going over and almost immediately the trench disappeared from sight as duckboards shot into the air. We were dead on target.

"Repeat," I shouted before the last round had arrived. Now for the other half of the trench.

"Switch two minutes right five rounds gun-fire." Some shells were falling short.

"Add twenty – three rounds gun-fire."

As the trench became visible again I saw the machine-gunner. He was covered in blood, terribly wounded, yet he was struggling to lift his gun back into position. I'd have to silence him.

"Left section only, return to Target one, five rounds gun-fire."

A minute or two passed as the guns were re-aligned. Through my glasses I could see Jerries running along the trench but the brave machine-gunner stayed at his post ...

Every Remembrance Day during the two minutes silence I can see him and recall the moment when he disappeared in a shower of rubble.

"Cease fire," I ordered.

As the dust cleared I noticed three or four men run from the trench round the corner of the hill. I let them go.

The Americans, having watched our infantry reach the enemy trench without opposition were delighted. I tried to put the incident of the machine-gunner out of my mind and think about Target II. On the telephone, I reported to Suthey that we had cleared the trench, but it would be half an hour before any of the escaping Jerries reached the road which was two miles away, beyond the hill. I added that few of them could have survived but those who did might panic others at the back of the hill. I was convinced there was a concentration of the enemy in that dead ground. Suthey said the guns would be ready with HE 103 fuse shells.

The Americans were doubtful about Target II; it was so far away and there would be only a few stragglers they said. I told them I was only going to put a volley on the first stretch, the hundred yards beyond the hill. I wouldn't risk following the enemy up the hill as we might damage our guns. That half hour seemed an age. As we scanned the road we looked beyond and spotted another which joined it further on. There was considerable activity here, traffic in both directions but it was well out of range. In good time I gave the order:

"Stand by for Target II."

At last they came. The road through the wire was black with retreating men. I could scarcely believe my eyes. It was like a crowd leaving a football match. "Prepare for salvo and five rounds gun-fire," I ordered.

I had to wait a few minutes for them to reach the target area. The first men, moving rapidly, were nearly there, probably thinking themselves lucky to escape. The Americans were yelling with excitement. I couldn't wait any longer. I gave the order.

"Fire!"

I shuddered and yet felt jubilant.

What happened next is a recurring nightmare.

I hear the salvo on its way. Judged by the report of the guns it is almost perfect. The range is six thousand yards, shells are all 103, the most efficient shell at this range.

What is happening? Grey-clad figures are falling in all directions disappearing in a cloud of smoke. I feel dazed, close my eyes and remember I am a soldier. There has been a pause. I pull myself together and order:

"Repeat!"

The smoke and dust have cleared. Men are lying all over the road – others have bolted into trenches alongside. Now two jump out of a trench and lift up a wounded man. I hear the roar of the second salvo – would to God I could stop it. The wounded man is raised up. I can see him clearly – a stretcher is brought. They are in the centre of the target ... please God stop the salvo ... but no – a direct hit ... the wounded man and the rescue party are no more. I weep. An American touches me gently on the arm. Again to duty. I'll take the guns off the wounded.

"Add one hundred, ten rounds rapid gun-fire."

I close my eyes and when I look again find that a heavy battery is now hammering the target. A man is hurtled fifty feet into the air.

"Cease fire," I order.

So often I had cursed the Hun and thirsted for revenge – but not this. I felt that never again could I direct guns to kill. Indeed, since that day at Morlancourt I have never even fired a shot-gun. The heavies continued to pound the distant target and the Americans accepted the excuse that our guns would be damaged if we continued to fire at extreme range. Now I had to endure their congratulations.

"Good Shooting, Gunner."

"Great, Buddy, great."

They were wild with glee.

The Commanding Officer expressed his thanks more formally but the others slapped me on the back and shook me by the hand before disappearing over the hill.

We picked up our telephone equipment and, winding up our wire, made our way down the hill. The signallers were thrilled with what they had seen and heard. Sad and subdued I said very little and I believe I even forgot to thank them for their excellent service. On the previous day because I couldn't shoot, I'd been seething with anger, now, having shot sucessfully, I was aghast at what I had done.

I called at the guns on my way to the mess and as I couldn't face talking about what had happened I simply told the sergeant they'd done an excellent job and that I'd come back later.

At the mess I sat down and wrote a very stilted report. I had barely finished when I was informed that the Colonel wanted me on the telephone. He congratulated me on a successful shoot – a credit to the Brigade. Then he mentioned that he was sending me on fourteen days' leave. Transport would arrive within the hour. Again? It was just over a week since I'd returned and there was bound to be a critical period ahead if we were to consolidate our position and make a further advance. We were desperately short of officers.

I shall never know why I was sent home.

11

Last Round

At Barras the weather was glorious and the crops ripe for harvesting. My brothers, delighted to see me again, soon had me hard at work. But despite the understanding of my loving wife and the peaceful beauty of the countryside – and to me nothing is more beautiful than those golden fields stretching down to the blue sea – still I was haunted by Morlancourt, by the needless slaughter of our men and by the horror of what I had done to the machine-gunner and the stretcher party. I didn't want to go back.

As my fortnight drew to a close, I applied for compassionate leave on the grounds that I was needed at home to help with the harvest. I was given another fortnight. We finished the harvest, then lent a hand on neighbouring farms, working by moonlight to complete the task before the weather broke.

By the middle of September my four weeks leave was at an end. Now learning to live with the memory of Morlancourt, I had become increasingly anxious about my friends in 377. I felt I had to go back as quickly as possible.

In fact during my absence the Brigade had taken an active part in many engagements, luckily suffering few casualties. I found them pulled back for a short rest period but there was an unusual spit and polish session in progress. Evidently a brass hat was coming next day to choose a section from the four batteries to act as a training unit for the Army School at St

Pol. Without delay I went to see if there was anything I could do for my section. Sergeant Gray had not only kept it in splendid condition but he had swopped some of our horses so that now we had beautifully matched teams, all black like my new charger.

Next day I found myself leading the left section round a ring for inspection. To our amazement we were chosen for the Army School. None of us was pleased. In fact Sergeant Gray was most upset, believing that the black horses which he had gone to so much trouble to acquire, had captured the attention of the brass hat. Two days later we reached the Army School at St Pol. We took no part in the instruction, only providing guns, horses and gunners to act as guinea pigs for cadets on training courses. We were continuously in exhibition trim, spit and polish to the extreme. We must have given satisfaction, for Suthey's many attempts to get us back to the Battery failed.

One episode at St Pol I recall with pleasure. The Commanding Officer was a football fanatic. His splendid team included Dodd, the Celtic player, and other internationals who happened to have arrived at the Army School. Our 377 section was expected to field a side against this formidable opposition. Thanks to Sergeant Gray we acquitted ourselves well and although we didn't win we scored early on and led up to half time. Even a goal scored against the CO's team was an indignity they had rarely suffered.

At last the Germans were near collapse and it became known that there were negotiations for a truce, and when news came through that the Armistice was to be signed on 11 November, we were ordered to rejoin the Brigade. We spent a night en route and on the evening of 10 November reached the Battery, which had been in action up to the end. We found our friends on the outskirts of Maubeuge about twenty miles from Mons where it had all begun in 1914.

There was great excitement and everyone was happy until 10 p.m. when a single shell came over and killed one of our men. There was more grief over this casualty than anything I can

169

remember – it seemed so unfair. No doubt some Jerry had fired the shell on his own initiative and it was unfortunate that it landed where it did but we were deeply upset that this should have happened when we thought the war was over.

Next morning the officers gathered in the bell tent which was our mess. At 11 o'clock Suthey answered the telephone. He turned to us and said:

"The war is over. Mount your horses."

"Mount your horses"? What an extraordinary command! But outside we found our grooms lined up with our chargers, and as soon as we were mounted followed Suthey at the gallop down the hill towards Maubeuge. We came to a halt by a narrow pontoon bridge which spanned forty yards of river. Suthey led the way across, turned left and trotted on towards the suburbs. Old men, women and children rushed out waving flags.

We were given an ecstatic welcome. As we reached a large dwelling a woman signalled to us to stop. We dismounted, tied up our horses, and followed her to a dilapidated garden at the back. There we saw an old man with a spade. He had already unearthed several bottles of cognac and wine. The ladies of the house found glasses and in no time we were celebrating the Armistice. After half an hour or more we bade our hosts farewell. With a great show of friendliness and many expressions of thanks in French and English, we untied our horses, mounted, and rode on. We had barely gone a hundred yards when an old man appeared from a doorway holding up a bottle of champagne. He waved to us to come in. We were off our horses in a flash.

I don't know how many times we partook of French hospitality that day, but I know it was growing dark as we gathered in a large room for our final celebration. We sang Scottish songs and ended up with "Scots Wha Hae". We had one English officer with us and when we bawled out "Lay the proud usurpers low", we downed him on the floor and piled on top as we continued to sing. The French were scared, I believe they feared we would kill him. At last Suthey decided that the celebration must end. He ordered us to mount and led us back to the pontoon bridge. I think we shared the same thought; it would be safer to allow our horses to make their own way over the rickety structure. We were lucky to reach the other side without mishap. What a party! We all thought Suthey should have been awarded a bar to his MC for his enterprise!

We trekked south-east to Peronne, this time taking our bell tents with us. There we received an order from Corps to carry out regular gun drill. The commanding officers made a very strong protest, explaining that while waiting for demobiliz-ation, the men were prepared to look after the guns, horses and equipment, but not take part in any military exercise as they now regarded themselves as ordinary citizens. The order was quickly withdrawn.

Waiting for demobilization, we kept ourselves busy and had no trouble in maintaining discipline. We played a great deal of football and 377 Battery, coached by Sergeant Gray, was unbeaten. In fact the Brigade team went on to challenge the winners of V Corps football competition and won.

One day I rode over to Gonnelieu with my groom. There were old iron stakes and rusty wire but the only sign of the guns we had left behind was a small scrap of camouflage net. Sixty years later I was to visit the site again, when a Frenchman led me to the cemetery and showed me the stump of a cross which had been knocked down in the First World War. To his astonishment, I described how this had come about when firing on the Germans hiding in the cemetery during the Battle of Cambrai.

In December 1918, we returned to Abbeville where the men were billeted in large farm buildings, part of a blacksmith's premises. Suthey and I stayed in the house. We had a wonderful Christmas Party and, being Scots, an even bigger one at Hogmanay. Suthey and I attended the Bonne Année of the blacksmith, his family and friends, including a number of blue-clad poilus.*

---

* A term used by British soldiers originally referring with affectionate respect to young French recruits.

It was a terrific celebration which took place in the loft of one of the barns. The table was groaning with food and drink. Everyone danced and everyone sang. Suthey, who possessed a good tenor voice sang "Passing By". Then after much applause there was a request for me to sing. I was dumbfounded; Suthey insisted I must make an effort. Suddenly I recalled singing 'Vive l'Amour' when a student but could only remember the first verse. I got to my feet and began "Let every good fellow now fill up his glass Vive la compagnie", and then on to the chorus, a succession of 'vive l'amours!' It was fantastic, the poilus jumped to their feet waving their arms.

"Encore, encore!"

I couldn't think of another verse but Suthey shouted:

"They don't understand a damned word. Sing the first verse again."

So I did just that, over and over again; the poilus now up on the table conducting the chorus. I'd never had such an audience.

Subsequently there were generous allocations of leave and I went home again at the end of January, returning to learn that Suthey and Smith had been demobilized and I was now in command. Someone told me that Smith intended to take a job with the Canadian Pacific Railway. Suthey returned to the ministry, in 1926 going to Dalmeny where, with characteristic enthusiasm, he restored St Cuthberts, now acknowledged as one of Scotland's most beautiful parish kirks.

Soon it would be my turn – on to the years ahead when images of war would return undimmed. As the two minutes silence ticks away on the day set aside for remembrance, I think of Watson at Cambrai, of Stevenson at Hangard, of a German machine-gunner and a stretcher party at Morlancourt. Armistice Day is not, as I once heard a young minister of the kirk proclaim to a congregation of war veterans, an outdated glorification of war. We recall our comrades and our enemy and we pray for peace.

My demobilization papers came through in March. When it

was time to go, I slipped quietly away unable to face the gunners, for the memories of all that had happened had come surging back in a great wave of emotion. The tears were streaming down my face.

Bibliography

Blaxland, Gregory: *Amiens 1918* (Frederick Muller, 1968)

Cooper, Bryan: *The Ironclads of Cambrai* (Souvenir Press, 1967 and Pan, 1970)

Edmonds, Brigadier-General Sir James E.: *Military Operations France and Belgium 1917 and 1918* Vol. III onwards (Macmillan, HMSO, 1935-47)

Ellis, J.: *Eye Deep in Hell* (Croom Helm, 1976; Fontana, 1977)

Falls, Cyril, Captain: *History of the 36th Ulster Division* (McCaw Stevenson and Orr; 1922)

Gibbs, Major A. Hamilton: *The Grey Wave* (Hutchinson, 1920)

Grey, Major W.E.: *The 2nd City of London Regiment (Royal Fusiliers) in the Great War* (Headquarters of the Regiment, 1929)

Keegan, John: *The Face of War* (Cape, 1976)

Middlebrook Martin: *The Kaiser's Battle, 21 March 1918, the First Day of the Spring Offensive* (Allen Lane, 1978)

Nichols G.H.F., Captain: *The 18th Division in the Great War* (Blackwood, 1922)

O'Neill, H.C.:*The Royal Fusiliers in the Great War* (Heinemann, 1922)

Pitt, Barrie: *1918 The Last Act* (Cassell, 1962)

Rutter, Owen (editor): *The History of the 7th Service Battalion The Royal Sussex Regiment* (The Times Publishing Company 1934)

Scott, Sir Arthur B. and Middleton Brumwell: *History of the 12th (Eastern) Division in the Great War* (Nisbet & Co, 1923)

Sparrow, W. Shaw: *The Fifth Army in March 1918* (John Lane, The Bodley Head, 1921)

Terraine, John: *Douglas Haig The Educated Soldier* (Hutchinson, 1963)

Terraine, John: *To Win a War, 1918 The Year of Victory*, (Sidgwick and Jackson, 1978)

Uniacke, Lt. General Sir Herbert: Papers, The Royal Artillery Institution

Wollcombe, Robert: *The First Tank Battle, Cambrai 1917* (Arthur Barker, 1967)